HIGH PEAK HIKES
– *walking in the foothills of the Peak District*

David Frith

Published by Sigma Leisure – an imprint of
Sigma Press, 1 South Oak Lane, Wilmslow, Cheshire SK9 6AR, England.

British Library Cataloguing in Publication Data
A CIP record for this book is available from the British Library.

ISBN: 1-85058-459-1

Typesetting and Design by: Sigma Press, Wilmslow, Cheshire.

Cover photograph: a view of Rowarth *(David Frith)*

Cover design: The Agency, Wilmslow

Maps: David Frith

Printed by: MFP Design and Print

Disclaimer: the information in this book is given in good faith and is believed to be correct at the time of publication. No responsibility is accepted by either the author or publisher for errors or omissions, or for any loss or injury howsoever caused. Only you can judge your own fitness, competence and experience.

Preface

This book is a celebration of many things – the countryside in the High Peak area of Derbyshire, its fascinating history, and – perhaps most important – the pleasures of rambling with a group such as our own New Mills group of the Ramblers Association.

The core of the book is a sixty-mile walk based on the local network of rights of way. It came about because 1995 was the sixtieth, Diamond Jubilee, Anniversary of the Rambler's Association. Nationally, the RA's 100,000 membership is shared between 51 geographical Areas which further sub-divide into 370 Groups. From the Rambler's Executive the call went out to the Areas and their constituent Groups, urging them to show initiative and produce a tangible lasting memorial to the Association.

Within the Manchester Area, New Mills Group, who have the Borough of High Peak as their patch, decided to create a circular walk, the length to be sixty miles, one mile for each year.

The walk passes through most of the High Peak parishes, using tracks and paths which will stand up to extra usage, visiting little-known attractions and enticing visitors from the 'honey pots' of the National Park. It passes through localities that are accessible by public transport and the route has flexibility. Each of the first four chapters covers approximately a quarter of the circuit, fifteen miles. Further each chapter breaks down into walks of six and nine miles. Hence the dedicated rambler can cover High Peak 60 in four consecutive days, or it may be walked in eight days, with each day's route alternating between six and nine miles.

To inaugurate High Peak 60, the public were invited to join with The Ramblers in walking the route over four days from May 5th to May 8th 1995.

Having used High Peak 60 to whet the appetite of the walking public a further 16 walks are described intended to introduce both local and visitor to the attractions of the Borough and the region's history. To complete the book, there is also an intriguing challenge walk, based on the historic chapels of the area.

David Frith

Contents

High Peak 60:
a 60-mile long-distance route in easy stages

High Peak 60, Section 1   **1**
– New Mills to Charlesworth and Glossop

High Peak 60, Section 2   **12**
– Glossop to Snake Inn and Hope

High Peak 60, Section 3   **20**
– Hope to Peak Forest and Buxton

High Peak 60, Section 4   **31**
– Buxton to Chapel en le Frith and New Mills

The Log of High Peak 60   **39**

More Walks in the High Peak

A High Peak Extension   **43**
Distance: up to 18 miles (29 km)

Glossop Go Round   **47**
Distance: 5 miles (8 km)

New Mills Circuit   **53**
Distance: 7 miles (11 km)

Phoside Foray   **58**
Distance: 5 milès (8 km)

Edale and the Ridge   64
Distance: 7 miles (11 km)

Edale to Fairholmes   71
Distance: 4 miles (6½ km)

Dambusters March   75
Distance: 8 miles (13 km)

Noe Return   81
Distance: 4 miles (6½ km)

Hope Hop   85
Distance: 4 miles (6½ km)

The Brindley Beat   91
Distance: 5 miles (8 km)

Grin Low and Ladmanlow   96
Distance: 4 miles (6½ km)

Discover Dove Holes   102
Distance: 3 miles (5 km)

Dove Holes to Chapel en le Frith   106
Distance: 2 miles (3 km)

Bagshaw and Bowden   110
Distance: 4 miles (6½ km)

Toddbrook and Taxal   115
Distance: 5 miles (8 km)

Brand New   120
Distance: 10 miles (16 km)

Interlude: Parishes, Paths and Partnership   127

The Ten Church Challenge
– a 21-mile circuit walk

Whaley Bridge to Whitehough   134
  Distance: 2½ *miles (4 km)*

Whitehough to Chinley   138
  Distance: ½ *mile (1 km)*

Chinley to Whiteknowle   140
  Distance: 1 *mile (1½ km)*

Whiteknowle to Town End   143
  Distance: 2 *miles (3 km)*

Town End to Bagshaw   145
  Distance: 2½ *miles (4 km)*

Bagshaw to Dove Holes   148
  Distance: 2½ *miles (4 km)*

Dove Holes to Combs   150
  Distance: 3 *miles (5 km)*

Combs to Fernilee   154
  Distance: 2 *miles (3 km)*

Fernilee to Kettleshulme   155
  Distance: 3 *miles (5 km)*

Kettleshulme to Whaley Bridge   159
  Distance: 2 *miles (3 km)*

High Peak 60, Section 1

New Mills to Charlesworth and Glossop

New Mills has two rail links into Manchester, one via Marple reaches Central Station *en route* to Sheffield. The Buxton to Stockport and Manchester railway uses Newtown Station – allow fifteen minutes to walk via Albion Road and Union Road to the Heritage Centre. The town centre bus station is serviced from Whaley Bridge, Macclesfield, Glossop, Marple, Stockport and Hayfield.

Dark Peak Map and Pathfinder Sheet 724 are required.

The route follows tracks and moorland paths, some farmland paths are not well-trodden.

From New Mills bus station [999855], on the corner of Albion Road and Hague Bar Road, the Heritage Centre is reached by descending from Rock Mill Lane. Opposite, a viewing platform gives a prospect down the vertical gorge wall to the mills and weir beside the Goyt.

Descend a flight of steps into the Torrs, make a left turn below Albion Road Bridge into mill ruins which are at the junction of the rivers Goyt and Sett. Their combined waters flow over a weir [001852]. By following the path left, the Sett valley is entered. A plaque on the rock wall commemorates the opening of the Torrs by Professor Graham Ashworth.

The path runs below the railway line. Continue at river level until steps climb to the bed of the former Hayfield railway line. On joining the track bed, look left to see the tunnel connecting back to New Mills Central. Ahead the Sett Valley Trail crosses the river. Pass

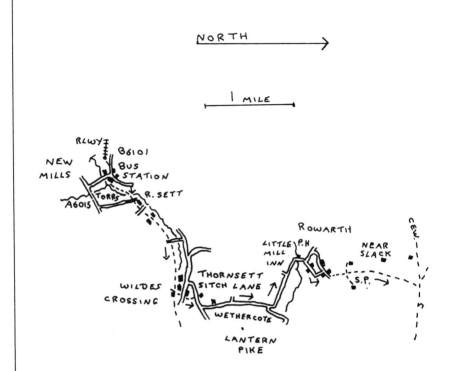

NEW MILLS TO GLOSSOP

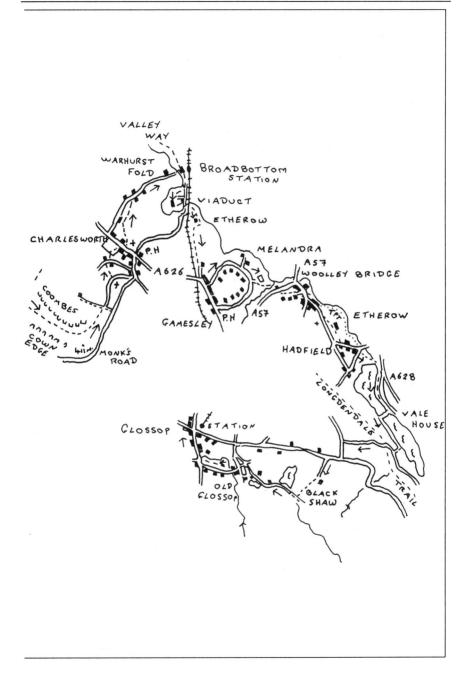

below Hyde Bank Road to the swimming pool. Keeping to the right of the Doctor's Group Practice, the trail runs to Church Lane. Cross the lane and head into and then out of an industrial valley where the railway bridge has been removed.

After crossing St. George's Road, the former rail track route skirts High Hills estate, passes over Watford Bridge Road and comes to High Hills Road on the Thornsett border [009866].

Look ahead towards Hayfield and Kinder Scout, to the north Thornsett School hugs the Brows with Highwalls Farm above. Continue along the Sett Valley Trail to the house at Wildes Crossing. Leave the trail, go down a cobbled road to two lower houses then cross the Sett to the end of Garrison Mills. Pass the mill end then the track bears left. Locate a cobbled brow which begins to ascend towards Sycamore Road. On the right, within twenty yards, a steep flight of steps is found, climb up onto the road [015870], cross the road and go through a gap in the opposite wall. A cobbled passage runs to the rear of the houses where a spring fills a trough. Go left up steps onto Sitch Lane.

Walk along the lane, which is partly-walled and partly-fenced. The route climbs to pass Bank Head Farm. The view stretches across Birch Vale with its quarry, and the straight line of Moorland Road is visible climbing past the TV Mast towards Chinley Churn. Looking back over New Mills, Lyme Cage stands on the horizon. The lane reaches a summit at 842 feet above sea level [020872] with extensive views across Hayfield onto Kinder and into the Downfall area.

From Sitch Lane go north passing Wethercotes, using a wide, walled track on the western flank of Lantern Pike. Ignoring the left-hand bridle path descending to Aspenshaw, continue into the Rowarth Valley with views west and north covering all the land from Alderley Edge to the hills above Bolton and Rochdale.

At an altitude of 970 feet above sea level, the track forks, [019884] take the track down into Rowarth, and the watershed of Rowarth Brook. The track descends over uneven slabs of bed rock. Laneside Farm is reached and Laneside Road followed around to the Little

Mill Inn. Across the vale is Long Lee Farm, written in Gothic script on the map to indicate a farmstead of great antiquity.

Little Mill Inn, dating from 1781, has a restored water wheel and may provide a useful refreshment stop. From the Inn, go to the corner of Hollinsmoor Road and take a rougher road, passing Brookside [011890], close to the stream. Pass two further cottages, go over a stile on the left to a flagged path, cutting the corner of the paddock to the telephone box. The path ends on Chapel Street, look for a memorial stone remaining from the Sunday School, "For Children Of All Denominations, AD 1824"

Rowarth village comprises two streets. It once had a Chapel and, until recently, a post office. Go along Chapel Street to the corner of Goddard Lane, one of the terraced houses is Drinkwaters Buildings, dated 1812. By Anderton House, on the right, turn to Poplar Farm and locate a sign post on the left, Peak and Northern sign 159, dating from 1973.

From the sign, the path runs up a passage into sloping fields. Follow the wall, go through a stone stile(see cover photograph), climb again to the finger post and pause to soak in the view [013897]. The sign is dedicated to S. Norman Ings, 1910-1982, Footpath Officer of New Mills and District Group of the Ramblers Association. Fingers point to Upper Rowarth, Rowarth, Back Rowarth, Hart Hill and Cown Edge, the direction we take. Climb up the path onto the brow of the hill, and over a series of crests making for the plateau. Kinder dominates the eastern skyline, but at times there are views into the north east onto Shelf and Bleaklow.

At the thousand-foot contour the moor levels, the ground is pock-marked from stone getting or coal working, an adjacent slope is called Coal Pit Hill. To the west stands Near Slack Farm. When the track forks, take the route north across rough pasture to a gate and stile, then across the plateau to a further stile. Continue until the Cown Edge Way is met [014910].

The Cown Edge Way has followed a bridle road commencing inside Chisworth parish and heading to Plainsteads. At this point our route and that of the Cown Edge Way run together. Over the fence and north east, look north into Longdendale and see the hills stretching over Arnfield to Alphin and Wilderness. Across the moorland, at twelve-hundred feet, the path runs to a wall. Crossing the wall, look down on Rocks Farm below the edge, enjoy further views across Monk's Road to Chunal, Harry Hut and Mill Hill.

Ignoring the chance to go onto the eastern headland, the path runs close to the plantation until the trees end and the walk reaches the western edge of the plateau, Coombes Rocks. Go onto the cliff top. Kestrels hunt off these windy ledges [019919]. The path follows the rim of a spectacular amphitheatre. Below is Mares Back, undulating landslips from post-glacial times. In the valley below lies Charlesworth, and beyond the apartments of Hattersley lies all of the Manchester conurbation, flanked by distant Lancastrian hills.

The path reaches a maximum altitude of 1282 feet before beginning a long, sweeping descent, almost parallel with Monk's Road, still in the company of the Cown Edge Way. The path runs down the spur, off the hill and comes to Coombes Farm drive. Go left over the cattle grid and through the stile. A path is followed down the Banks, keeping close to Back Lane, through a series of stiles until the path swings back onto Back Lane, a field away from the Independent Church, 'Top Chapel' [009924].

Here, carefully descend the steep grass and gorse hill side, following the wall, over two stiles, onto Boggard Lane. Reaching the lane, turn towards Charlesworth. Pass two cottages on the left and step down off the lane onto a lower drive at the first house on the right. Cross, go through a stile and follow the high hedge to a stile in the corner of the recreation ground.

Once on the playing field, head for Marple Road, passing swings and slides until the A626 is met [004926]. If the day's walking is to end here, there is a bus service along this road, linking Hazel Grove to Glossop via Marple (not Sundays). If Marple Road is followed for a quarter of a mile into Charlesworth, buses run hourly to Manchester, Hyde and Glossop. For a return to New Mills either go to and change buses in Marple, or on Sundays catch a bus to New Mills from Glossop.

If you are continuing to Glossop on foot, exit from the recreation ground onto Marple Road, turn right, north east, and walk to the Springfield estate. Opposite a path commences beside a small housing development.

Starting in Charlesworth, the A626 Marple Road forms a staggered junction with Town Lane and Long Lane. The junction is guarded by The Grey Mare and The George and Dragon. Go south west along Marple Road, passing St. John's Church and the Conservative Club. Look on the left for an estate, Springfield. Opposite a small housing development is being completed on the site of Old Foundry Mill.

The footpath runs down the north side of the development to a gate and stile. Once in the meadow, head to the power line pole then follow the overhead wires west. The path, visible in parts, runs to bushes and crosses a series of dry valleys [002927]. After the last depression, go along the line of bushes on the valley rim, aiming for the tree at the wall end. Turn and follow the wall and fence to a stile in the corner. The stile is made visible with a splash of white paint.

Over the stile, and aiming north of west, go to the tree with a white waymark, then straight across to a stile over a low wall, again marked with white paint. In line with the previous section of path, cross the next field aiming for a silver birch on the flank of a wooded gully. Reach the birch, descend to a footbridge, then pass out of the gully into a thistle field. Note a white sighting board on the bush behind. Now look across the field towards the enlarged house, and spot another sighting board. Aiming for this, cross the field to a bridge over the ditch and, after a precarious stile, join Woodseats Lane [995928].

Turn down the lane, passing Blue Marl, Hunters Gate and Howard Cottage. There is little traffic, and views across to Broadbottom and down river to Werneth Low. From Warhurst Fold, Woodseats Lane runs as a narrow track to the Etherow at Warhurst Fold Bridge. Cross the river and enter Tameside [993936].

Two long distance routes are met here. One path, the Valley Way, commences at Vernon Park. It follows the Goyt to Otterspool and enters Chadkirk. Upstream of Romiley, the Valley Way takes in

Etherow Country Park before reaching Broadbottom, *en route* to Woolley Bridge. The Trans Pennine Trail, an initiative to traverse England with a route comprising old railways and canal towing paths, may pass this way. The Longdendale Trail is one completed section. A recent addition is the Tameside Trail, opened in August 1994, following the forty mile perimeter of Tameside Borough.

The route of High Peak 60 turns upstream on the Broadbottom bank and runs through the visible and identifiable ruins of Broad Mills. A plaque commemorates the opening of Valley Way, September 1992. Reaching the houses at Lymefield Terrace, turn to cross the mill feed and reach Lymefield Warden Centre, information and toilets [996936]. Crossing the car park, the children's information route heads through shrub land to the railway viaduct. Reach the bridge at Lower Market Street and cross the Etherow at Besthill Bridge, back into High Peak.

Turn under the viaduct, beside the right-hand pier discover a path scrambling up the bank into shrubs. It levels out and runs up the gorge, over a stile onto the edge of pasture land, keep close to the trees, treading a flagstone path. In time another stile is crossed, go down through the trees, the path is on a narrow terrace above road and river. On reaching the mill ruin at Botany, go down onto the track and forward to the house.

Go through the white gate below the house and into the yard [999941], look right for an innovative footpath sign. Cross the stile and, close to the pond, follow the fence and hedge towards Robin Wood Farm. The railway line in a cutting alongside, reach Gamesley Bridge and join the A626 at a terrace of houses. Take a passage on the left onto Gamesley Estate, join Melandra Castle Road and skirt around the estate. Pass the bowling green, the drive to Melandra Farm and arrive at Melandra Castle [009950].

In 78 AD Agricola, Roman Governor of Britain, commissioned a fort at Melandra. Known to the Romans as Ardotalia, derived from the river's name, the garrison housed Frisian Auxiliaries within wooden defences. Between 98 – 117 AD the fort was rebuilt in stone, surviving until 140 AD when it was burnt down and abandoned.

Within the fifteen feet high walls were six timber barrack blocks. Outside the wall, a civil settlement developed, complete with 'mansio' or staging house for travellers and mails. The name Melandra is eighteenth century. Crude archaeological digs unearthed remnants of oak posts blackened with age. The Greek for *black oak* soon corrupted to melandra.

The fort had a watch tower at each corner. From the base of the north tower a path descends to Melandra Road. Once on the road cross Glossop Brook close to its confluence with the Etherow and follow the road to the A57 at Brookfield [011953]. Across the road is the route of the Waterside Goods Line which opened on October 10 1879, taking freight from sidings on the Manchester-Sheffield railway, at Gamesley, to mills at Woolley Bridge and Waterside. The line closed on February 18 1964. Bridges have gone and the track may become a section of the Trans Pennine Trail. Currently, the track between Melandra and Woolley Bridge has been bulldozed to provide land for yet more houses. If the Trail has not been established, walk north with the A57, passing the Spring Tavern, to Woolley Bridge, then into Woolley Bridge Road and past the factory units. The route of the rail bed is met opposite Waltkin Avenue on the right [011960]. Walk along the rail route, passing the mills, onto the Etherow bank. One day it will be possible to follow the river's side upstream to Tintwistle Bridge, for the present, leave the railway track by crossing onto Woolley Bridge Road, opposite St. Charles Hall.

Walk east along Woolley Bridge Road beside the security fence at Nestle until the fence veers away from the road. The path follows the fence onto Waterside. Reaching Waterside, go downhill, noting the high wall on the left which was once the frontage of mill workers' cottages. Door and window lintels still survive [020966].

Close to Tintwistle Bridge, a road descends from the right. On the corner there is a trough marked "Manchester Corporation Water Works 1879". Here there are Trans Pennine Trail signs. Go right into Goddard Lane and through the gate onto a track rising to Bottoms Reservoir. The route of High Peak 60 rises to the dam crest, enters Tintwistle and crosses the overflow [023972]. Pause and look down the spillway into a gauge basin which feeds the Etherow a predetermined volume of water required by the downstream mills. Over the bridge, on the right, a monumental valve house bears the Manchester coat of arms. On the side is a tablet listing various Acts of Parliament passed in the years 1847, 1848, 1863 and 1865. These enabled the Manchester Corporation Water Works to impound the Etherow with five dams, a construction work which lasted 29 years from 1848 to 1877. The memorial lists those who served on the committee. The engineer through out the construction was John Frederick Bateman FRS.

Walk up the drive towards the gates. Before the gate, a path descends to cross the bywash then follows the channel up the valley. At the water-sports centre this path crosses the drive and runs along the five-hundred foot contour, through the pine plantation onto Valehouse embankment [031974]. Cross the second dam, after the bridge turn north east on the reservoir side track, passing below Valehouse Farm and enjoying views to Tintwistle Knarr and Nell's Pike.

This rough road drops into a clough, turns a bend and rises up to a tarmac road. There is a bench on the junction [038975], and an access point onto the Longdendale Trail. For this hike the route follows the road as it climbs to cross the Longdendale Trail. Walk along a quiet lane to Padfield Main Road [036966]. Walk with Padfield Main Road between the two reservoirs at Runal Intake onto Woodhead Road, B6105. On joining the road, at 869 feet above sea level, turn south towards Glossop. In two hundred yards take a left-hand track to Blackshaw Farm.

Close to the farm the track forks, take the path on the right, through gates and stiles, into fields close to the ruins of Lower Blackshaw. A track runs through fields above Swineshaw Reservoir until a plantation is reached [045958]. Follow the wall to the foot of Swineshaw embankment and pass below the dam. See the cataract of water flowing off Broom Hill then pass Keyford Cottage and Broomside until Cote Lodge is reached. Beyond this second reservoir, the track runs past Shire Hill Hospital the former Glossop workhouse, here the road forks. Take the drive to Swineshaw Water

Treatment plant, down steps to houses on Blackshaw Road and beneath the first high-rise dwellings. Follow the road slightly uphill, looking left for the traffic free ramp of Dunne Lane. Descend, looking left for the former butcher's with a stone bull's head and lintel carvings depicting the tools of the trade. Emerge onto Wellgate between The Wheatsheaf and The Bull's Head [042949]. Go forward into Church Street and down this well-preserved street whose Elizabethan cottages lie within the shadow of All Saint's Church. Look left to see the village cross which dates from the time when this settlement was the town and today's Glossop was Howard Town. Walk down Church Street South to The Queen's, from where the hike to Hope commences.

To reach Glossop: cross Shelf Brook into Manor Park Road. Opposite the post office a wall gap gives access to Manor Park. Walk the path through the open spaces to the tennis courts. Cross the park railway and to the stone pavilion [041944]. From here skirt the bowling greens until the path descends to a footbridge and exits onto Corn Street. Go down to High Street East, A57 [039941] follow it west into the centre of Glossop.

2

High Peak 60, Section 2

Glossop to Snake Inn and Hope

Glossop is served by trains from Manchester six days a week. Frequent buses run into Manchester, either through Hyde or Ashton. Daily buses run to Stockport via Hayfield and New Mills. Monday to Saturday a service links with Charlesworth and Marple to Hazel Grove. Summer services run to Huddersfield, Castleton and Buxton.

Dark Peak Map required.

The route is rough and wet. It crosses exposed moorland so go suitably equipped.

Reaching Old Glossop from the town centre, you will pass The Norfolk Arms [035941], beside the traffic lights. Go along High Street East until Shelf Brook is met. Go up Corn Street, which is on the left, to a footbridge into Manor Park. Once in the park, walk uphill, passing bowling greens and tennis courts. A path across open parkland leads to a gateway into Manor Park Road. A few yards north, Shelf Brook is crossed again, here stands The Queen's [042947].

From The Queen's at Old Glossop, walk east along Shepley Street, crossing the junction with Blackshaw Brook which flows in company with Wesley Street on the right. Shepley Street follows the brook past the mills towards Tan Yard Farm. Shelf Brook, in this length, has recently been dredged and weirs have been provided to break the energy of flood waters. This has encouraged the deposition of shingle which would otherwise make shallow the lower stream channel. At the end of the mill the brook passes through a boulder trap, arresting the journey of the largest of the water borne rocks.

Heading towards Mossy Lea, the bridle road runs between Shire Hill and Lightside. The first building on the right at Tan Yard is the Colin Hugh's camping barn, a venture supported by the Countryside Commission. Passing Tan Yard, the track continues up the valley. Small Clough flows down off Glossop Low and the track eventually reaches the bridges at the confluence of Shelf and Yellowslacks Brook [061946].

The route over the moors from here is called Doctor's Gate, the name is used on the signpost at the gate. The Peak and Northern sign details the walk as running by Doctor's Gate Roman Road to Snake Inn and Alport Bridge. From the gate, the track climbs up towards Shelf Benches. The view back west embraces Mossy Lea Farm, a small reservoir and the bulk of Shire Hill. Climb up the track, following the wall to a barn. Here a second Peak and Northern sign, dating from 1950, stands at a path junction. From here the path runs level up the valley, the sides becoming increasingly high and steep. In time a ruined wall is crossed, the obvious route descends towards the brook and follows it upstream. If you go forward and keep level, a much narrower path is found which runs at a height above the stream until it descends and splashes through a swamp, joining the main track close to Little Clough.

The obvious path now runs upstream to a footbridge [075941], over the Ambler Memorial bridge and up a wet, rocky incline to reach Birchen Orchard Clough, draining off Coldharbour Moor. To the north lies high ground comprising the tops of James Thorn and Shelf Stones, the stream cascading down between the two is Ashton Clough. Three wrecked aircraft, a Superfortress, a Lancaster and a Dakota, lie within a mile of each other around those moorland heights.

The path levels, turns the corner of the hill, and, now facing south, rises to cross Rose Clough. Shelf Brook can be seen flowing out of Crooked Clough, ahead is the flank of Old Woman. Rising again, the route fords Urchin Clough then zigzags up the corner of the moor,

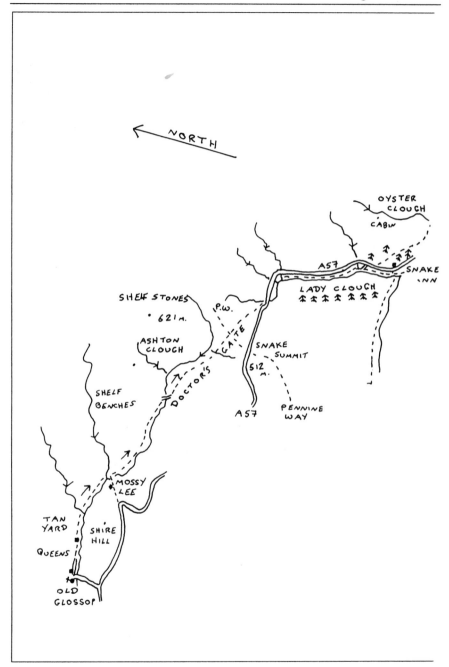

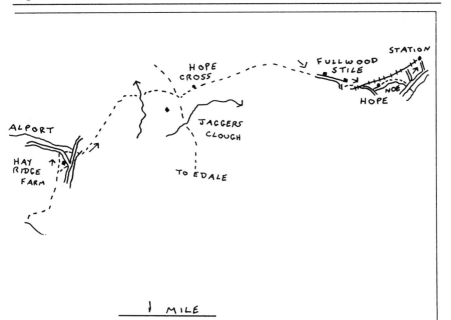

1 MILE

GLOSSOP TO HOPE

finally climbing through a shallow shale ravine to the summit of Old Woman [089934].

From Old Glossop it is been almost three miles, climbing a little over 1000 feet. The path across the watershed to Doctor's Gate Culvert can be less obvious in poor weather. On the level top of the moor the route follows a section of paving reputed to be a Roman Road. In reality it is an early pack road over the hill. True, the Romans, *en route* to Brough from Melandra, crossed these hills. Their route probably crossed Mill Hill at Moss Castle and descended the Ashop to Oyster Clough. The name Doctor's Gate was first used in 1627, when the full title was Doctor Talbot's Gate possibly named after Dr. John Talbot, illegitimate son of the Earl of Shrewsbury and vicar at Glossop between 1494 to 1550

Across Old Woman the path rises a little further to 1686 feet above sea level and meets the Pennine Way. Here is a change of drainage, the walk leaves the Mersey Basin and enters the gathering grounds of the Derwent draining through Trent and Humber to the North Sea. South of Doctor's Gate one can usually see the traffic crossing the Snake summit. The path runs alongside the paving before ending in a bog. Aiming south east, the path reaches a stream at the head of Lady Clough and, after fording the brook, turns south to join the A57 at Doctor's Gate Culvert [096929].

Joining the road at Peak and Northern sign 58, dating from 1938, walk down the road for a quarter of a mile, approaching the culvert where Upper North Grain drains off Over Wood Moss. Where the road side wall ends and a tubing fence commences, cross the fence and descend into Lady Clough, noting an inclined causeway running to the confluence of Upper North Grain and Lady Clough. A close look at the Ordnance Survey map shows a streamside path, this is visible and may have been an extension from Doctor's Gate. The first stream is crossed on an ancient clapper bridge, the next stream, Nether Fork Grain, is forded and ahead is the edge of the forest. In a few yards a quality stile is reached and a sign 'Lady Clough Forest Walk' welcomes the route into the woodland [103926].

The Forest Walk is a well-built pathway. Following Lady Clough, the path descends to the stream side, don't cross the bridge, enjoy the route which rises and falls through a dense, dark pine forest. In time it descends stone steps and runs by the stream to the confluence of Lady Clough with Birchin Clough. Cross the plank bridge over the tributary, and continue to a well-built concrete bridge. Here there is a choice of route.

If the intention is to terminate the walk at The Snake Inn, continue down the stream to its confluence with the River Ashop. A well-used path, heading down the Ashop, soon rises to join the A57 close to The Snake Inn. Should one wish to take a traditional route to Hayfield, some six miles further, again follow the Lady Brook down to the Ashop. From the Ashop junction turn west, taking the Snake Path through the Ashop Valley back over the Mersey Watershed into the shale ravine of Wiliam Clough and down into the Kinder Valley.

To continue with the High Peak 60 through to Hope, from the concrete bridge over the Lady Brook [108913], take the forest road away from the stream up onto the A57. Cross the main road and going slightly north, locate the start of the Oyster Clough path, commencing at Peak and Northern signpost 56, dating from 1924, replaced in 1993.

On summer Sundays and bank holiday Mondays, buses from Manchester, Glossop and Castleton cross over the Snake Pass, enabling the walk from The Snake Inn to Hope to be enjoyed by those wanting a less strenuous hike.

Leave the Snake Road at the Peak and Northern Footpath Sign pointing to Oyster Clough, found a mile north of The Snake Inn, beside the A57 [109911]. The path climbs through the plantation. In a clearing there is a jumble of fallen rock at the base of Dinas Sitch Tor. The walk tends uphill to a stile at the top of the forest, and out onto Alport Moor. Still climbing, the track constructed to reach Oyster Clough cabin, forks at a wooden stump. Walk the path heading alongside the forest fence. Pause and look around, south and west across the Ashop Trench are valleys and crags, the highest ground comprises Kinder Edge coming to a climax at Fairbrook Naze. As the path runs along the rubble remnant of the woodland wall, a further Peak and Northern sign tells the walker to stay beside the wall. Following this advice, the path descends to Oyster Clough, fords the stream and climbs out of the valley onto Cowms Moor [123900].

The path through the fields is marked as it descends slowly towards Hayridge Farm. Interestingly, there is a short section of paved path before the National Trust Cowms Moor sign is met and a stile crossed. The route now gives views south onto the Seal Edges. The paths climbing up to Gate Side Clough are visible, and ahead views stretch beyond the Alport onto the wooded ridge between the Ashop and the Derwent.

Approach Hayridge down a sunken track. The walk diverts around the north side of the farmstead to reach the lane running up to Alport Farm. From the side of the lane, a short path descends towards the River Alport, meeting the A57 at Alport Bridge, signpost 106. Cross the Snake Road, go through the gate and down to the junction of the Alport and the Ashop [141894]. Cross the Ashop, either by ford or footbridge, then walk the bridle road running close to Upper Ashop Farm. A wide track skirts the foot of Blackley Hey, ascend a rough road with a steady gradient to the fording of Blackley Clough [155882]. When the short climb beyond the ford is tackled, a different view is had. The wooded ridge dividing the Derwent and the Noe is visible. This, if followed, would ascend to the summit of Win Hill. High Peak 60 passes close to Crookstone Barn and reaches Hope Cross. There is a stone pillar at the cross roads of pack horse routes, its capstone identifies four destinations: Sheffield, Edale, Hope and Glossop. There is date of 1737 [161874].

Descending the Roman Road to Fullwood Stile Farm, the flanks of Lose Hill can be seen across the valley, a road and railway skirting its feet. At Fullwood Stile go into the farm yard, turn to the right [171848], around a corner and over a stile on the right to walk through fields parallel with railway sidings. The sidings hold the cement trains which serve the kilns connected to the distant tall chimney. The path becomes a lane. Turn right to pass below the railway, pass the Burrell memorial signpost and continue to a house on the left, Mill Barn [172840]. A sign points to Brough, take the track running downstream from Killhill Bridge. Follow the Noe to a derelict water-wheel. At the house turn away from the river, pass the conservatory up steps to enter the field. The path runs beside the Noe to Station Road at Netherhall Bridge [175833]. On reaching the A625, go east, passing Aston Road, to the station approach and up to the platform for trains either to Sheffield or Manchester [181832].

3

High Peak 60, Section 3

Hope to Peak Forest and Buxton

Hope has daily trains from Manchester, Marple, New Mills and Sheffield. Buses pass through the village *en route* to Sheffield and Castleton. Summer buses run to Chesterfield and Manchester.

Dark Peak and White Peak maps required.

Varied route, farmland and wet moorland, several steep ascents.

From Hope Station [181832] a drive runs to Station Road, the A625,
which is followed west, crossing the Noe at Netherhall Bridge. Enter
Hope at the village church. Go into the church yard and between
graves and well-trimmed trees to the doorway, with gargoyles, niche
and finial. After a visit to the interior to St. Peter's, take the path
heading south from the door to the Vicarage, and down onto the
lane.

Walk down to the bridge over Peakshole Water. Cross the bridge,
noting the restored Pinfold [172834], and walk away from Hope.
Pass the junction with Eccles Lane and follow Pindale Road, looking
on the right for the Kitty Smith memorial sign which marks the
commencement of the Castleton path. Through the first field the
route is surfaced as it follows the brook. Walk past trees to the
railway serving the cement works, then on through fields and over
stiles until once more the walk runs beside Peakshole Water. It
finally rejoins the A635 on the outskirts of Castleton. When the road
is met note a Peak and Northern sign dating from 1908 at an altitude
of 592 feet [154831].

Head on into Castleton, past the bus station and toilets, turning the corner at the bank. After passing the school, ignore the right turn along the main road, instead continue up the street, passing the rear of St. Edmund's Church, to the cenotaph in the open space before the Youth Hostel [150828]. Turning left, Bargate leaves the village. Look for a sign pointing the way into Cave Dale at the start of the Limestone Way.

The path passes cottages then enters the steep, narrow passage between limestone cliffs. At the gate, the dale widens, sheep-cropped grass cloaks the near vertical walls. Overhanging limestone cliffs make the scene more dramatic, and in the wider part various shallow caves can be explored [149824]. Look back and see the keep of Peveril Castle perched on the cliff edge.

Climbing higher up the dale, the rocks once again squeeze the path and the surface is rough. Go through a gate and there is a change in geology. The dark rocks to the left are volcanic in origin. The path follows a dry valley out onto the moor. The view back stretches across Hurd Low to Rowter Farm and Mam Tor. Deep below this limestone upland are pot holes and lead mines. Many of the old mines are now opencast, and are not worked for galena, but for either fluorspar or barytes. From Castleton there is a steady climb of eight hundred feet in two miles to reach a track crossing the moor [136813].

Ahead the sign points towards Peak Forest. The bridle path follows the wall, west of south, to ground disturbed by mining activity. The first path junction above Oxlow Rake is ignored. Go over the stile and, still beside the wall, ascend to a high point of 1400 feet, passing a circular pond before taking the level path [132804] passing former Starvehouse Mine. As the path commences its descent, walls enclose the route. As Dick Lane it runs to the house at The Cop, down past West View into Old Dam Lane.

Turn west along the tarmac road past Brocktor Farm, locate a stile and gate on the left, before Stonebrack [124793]. The path skirts the garden wall on a recently diverted line, then crosses the wall and follows the wall, aiming towards the A623. Keep to the wall side,

HOPE TO PEAK FOREST

1 MILE

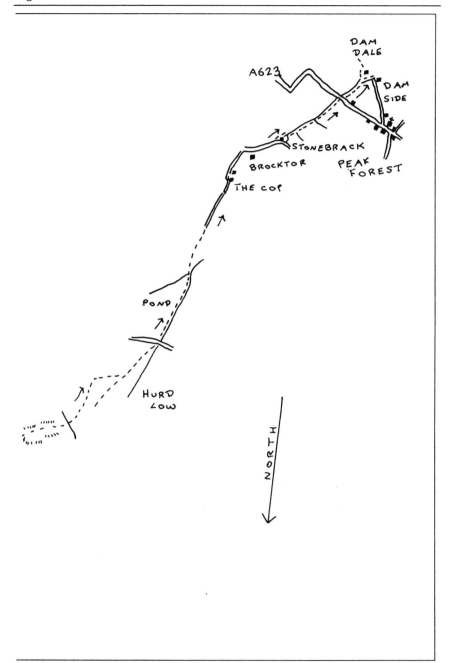

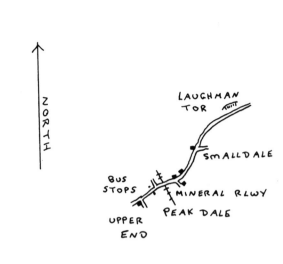

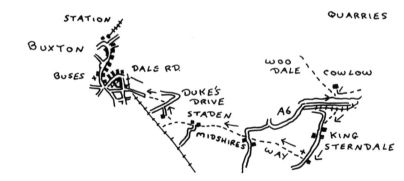

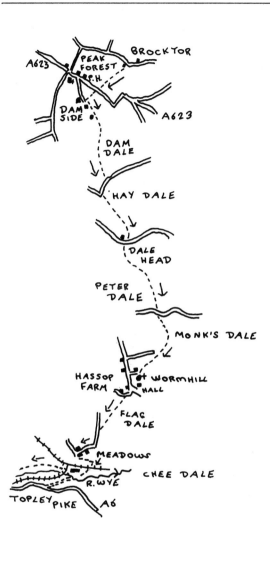

PEAK FOREST TO BUXTON

finally rising slightly to join the road, Hernstone Lane on the outskirts of Peak Forest [118789].

A short distance north west lies the village centre, The Devonshire Arms and the Church of Charles, King and Martyr. Buses link the village to Manchester and Chesterfield on Friday, Saturday, Sunday and Bank Holiday Mondays. Other infrequent local buses are available, consult the Peak District Timetable Handbook.

Requiring public transport? If you are prepared to go the extra mile, a road walk of less than two miles leads south from Peak Forest to the hamlet of Smalldale. This road follows close to the line of the roman road, Batham Gate. The Smalldale road climbs to a high point atop Laughman Tor [102779] then descends through Smalldale to the railway bridge at former Peak Dale Station. It is interesting to pause here, watching the freight trains hauling limestone and roadstone along the line through Doveholes Dale. Over the bridge, from the corner[091768], an hourly bus service runs, seven days a week to Stockport and Buxton. Missed the bus? Then follow the railway directions along Doveholes Dale road into Dove Holes for additional buses or the railway station.

Walking on to Buxton from Peak Forest, the village centre can be avoided. When the path from Stonebrack joins the main road, cross the road. A path opposite follows the wall to one of two Peak and Northern signposts. From the first sign post, No. 222, descend [116788] towards the second one, No. 223, situated on the centre of the dam. Shortly before Mill Cottage, built in the lee of the dam, however, go over the limestone wall and head down Dam Dale, making to the trees east of Dam Dale Farm [118785].

Making a separate walk of the route from Peak Forest to Buxton, Peak Forest will have been reached either by bus or by retracing the walk through Smalldale from the bus stop at Peak Dale Station.

Peak Forest straddles the A623. The village reading room, on the corner of the Smalldale road, dates from 1880, a little to the east is the Church of Charles, King and Martyr. The original Church dating from 1657, founded by the Countess of Devonshire, had the distinction of being the 'Gretna Green' of the Peak District. The minister, acting as surrogate to the Bishop, joined many runaway couples in marriage. The Fleet Street Marriage Act of 1753 put an end to this tradition.

Between the two stands an old school house, the present primary school stands opposite, close to The Devonshire Arms. On the right, after the burial yard, runs Damside Lane. This is followed to Damside Farm [115788].

The lane passes through the yard at Damside Farm and goes onto the dam, which once held water for a corn mill. On the downstream side of the dam, Mill Cottage remains. Cross the dam, passing the Peak and Northern Footpath sign post 223, dating from 1990, in memory of Arthur and Edna Hodkinson.

Across the dam and over a stile in the limestone wall, close to the side of Mill Cottage, the path becomes more difficult to follow because of cattle, but goes south to trees beside Dam Dale Farm. Go over a stile, through a kissing gate below the trees at the side of the farm and walk down Dam Dale, crossing the line of Batham Gate Roman road, which is not visible on the ground.

Dam Dale is a dry valley, and the flat, wide valley floor is divided into small fields, some with fodder barns. The path follows the 1000 foot contour. At the end of the dale, climb the stile, noting the large 'through stone' of crinoidal limestone [119774]. An unsurfaced road brings the Limestone Way into the valley, now called Hay Dale. A few yards down the lane cross over a stile, the path leads into a grove of trees.

Follow the avenue of trees down Hay Dale. When the trees end look on the east of the path for the remnant of a small mine, which was possibly once used for extracting fluorspar. There is a fissure into which a rail track descends. Grooves have been worn into the sleepers by the steel hawser which pulled the tubs out of the mine. These would be emptied by inverting them in a tumbler, the base of which can be seen beside the mine floor.

The valley continues to a tarmac road at Dale Head [122765] where a stream of water flows into a pond. The valley alternates between being wide with a grassy floor, and narrow with craggy walls and a stony surface.

Below Dale Head the valley is known as Peter Dale, which is wide with a grassy floor then narrows to a rocky pass. It widens and narrows until widening again as it reaches the Tideswell to Hargate Wall road and enters Monk's Dale National Nature Reserve [130752].

On reaching the road, go west for a few yards, over a stile and climb up out of the valley, heading for Wormhill. The path reaches level farmland and is joined by a bridle way, together they run to a junction of tracks [128746]. This high point on the plateau gives views south to the hills behind Taddington and east towards the Wye at Miller's Dale.

The track to Wormhill runs south west between walls, note the remnants of a stone kerb. Wide fields are reached, and the path heads for a stile. In its final stages the footpath runs west down the centre of a long, wide field, aiming for the farm. At the farm gate the path is led off south onto a track which, when followed past Holly House, reaches the gate of St. Margaret's Church, Wormhill [124742].

The church, dedicated to St. Margaret of Antioch, dates from 1864, Wormhill having becoming a parish in 1859. Unique in having a helmet steeple, its peel of 6 bells, one of the lightest in the country, has not been rung for several years as they await restoration. Transepts were added in 1904. Wormhill is mentioned in the Domesday survey and was once within the parish of Tideswell, under the Diocese of Lichfield. A chapel of ease existed from the thirteenth century, and it was here that the Rev. William Bagshaw, Apostle of the Peak, preached in 1660. Look in the burial yard for a sundial dated 1670, giving the latitude as 53^0 30'.

Go back onto the track, which is followed to the village well. On the well is a plaque, dated 1875, in memory of James Brindley, civil engineer, born in this parish 1716 AD. Wormhill's well dressing is the last week in August. On the other side of the well, a limestone block bears a further Brindley plaque, positioned here in 1989 by the Institute of Civil Engineers assisted by I.C.I. Chemicals and

Polymers. After trying out the stocks, turn south down the tarmac road as if towards Miller's Dale. Passing Wormhill Hall on the left, look on the right for Hassop Farm. A stile on the right after the farm drive gives access to the yard, go to the gate past the buildings on the left, into a rear yard and up to a finger post [123739]. Through the narrow gate, secured by a turn button, walk to a second gate then south west to the rim of Flag Dale and down the path onto the dale floor.

Climb the steep path out of the dale, over the stile and up the sloping field into two large meadows where the path is indistinct. The land to the west is bordered by a quarry road and a belt of timber. There is a sign post where the path joins the surfaced track [117733]. From here to Meadows the original track, churned by cattle, runs parallel to the quarry road. It's easier and cleaner to take the tarmac route to the farm, and keep with the track, passing between barns and houses, until the lane turns sharp right. From this corner go onto a left-hand track which runs to a grassy headland with views down onto the Wye at Blackwell Mill [114729].

A steep twisting path descends towards the river. Ignore any off shoots, and go down the path until it runs below the former Miller's Dale railway and reaches the Wye upstream of Chee Dale. Turn up river to cottages at Blackwell Mill, don't cross, but continue upstream to the pump house. After this building, a path through comfrey and butter-burr runs towards the railway. Pass below the line in a tunnel, [111727] which is partly obstructed by bushes, then climb a steep path which crosses a disused railway cutting on a sloping bridge of slippery timbers. The path climbs steeply to give views of the Tunstead Quarries. At the hill top go over a stile and follow a path between bushes and a fence until views open out across Topley Pike. At the end of the woods, go over a stile into the fields and continue up the valley. Down below is the Wye, the A6, and the quarry railway heading towards Buxton. The rail connection into Topley Pike Quarry can also be seen.

At another stile [102726] the path leaves the fields for the valley rim and keeps close to the wall, heading for Cow Low Farm. After a final stile, descend steeply to the river at the foot of Woo Dale and cross the Wye onto the A6.

Turning west, a steep path climbs to the railway [098724]. Over the mineral line the path climbs again to reach a track running into Kingsterndale. Look at the old cross in the centre of the hamlet, a faint inscription reads, "This ancient market cross was repositioned by the parish in commemoration of the coronation of His Majesty King George..." Which King and when are difficult to read. From Kingsterndale, walk down the lane, past Christ Church and the Old School House, until on the right stands a Midshires Way marker [092716]. Walk with this long distance path through the flat farmland, stiles and waymarkers until the path reaches Highcliff Farm at Cow Dale.

The final waymark is on a post by a large slurry tank. Go forward onto the road, turn right to the seat and left on a track beside another farm, still part of the Midshires Way running to Staden [082720].

Walk into Staden past a stable yard with a date of 1829 on a lintel. At Staden go right and take the track [074722] skirting around Staden Low which turns towards Duke's Drive and gives views forward to the elegant railway viaduct. On the right a track descends through a farmstead onto Duke's Drive at Limetree Caravan Park [068725]. Cross the road and go slightly right, up the bank to a stile. The path follows the wall and fence away from Duke's Drive. Go through a gate on the left and across the rugby pitch [065727] into a drive running between allotments to the railway bridge. Cross the line, pass Crowestones into Byrom Street and take the second right, Bennet Street, down onto Dale Road. Turning left into Dale Road, note the Roll of Honour for Bennet Street men on the corner house gable [060731]. Walk along Dale Road past St. Mary's Church to the traffic lights. Turn right along High Street to Market Place [058732] with its cafes, toilets and bus stops.

4

High Peak 60, Section 4

Buxton to Chapel en le Frith and New Mills

Buxton market ground has bus stops for services running to Sheffield,
Hanley, Bakewell, Matlock, Derby and Nottingham. Local buses connect to Longnor, Hartington, Tideswell and Chinley. Another frequent
service runs via Whaley Bridge to Disley and Stockport. The station,
with hourly trains to Manchester, lies fifteen minutes away. It is
reached by descending Terrace Road past Spring Gardens and walking up The Quadrant.

White Peak and Dark Peak map required.

Field paths, lanes, moorland, steep ascents and a canal towing path

Leaving Buxton market ground, High Peak 60 descends Hall Bank
from the west side of the former town hall. To one side are the
Terrace Slopes where meteorological equipment records the local
climate. At the base of the slopes stands The Crescent, St. Anne's
Well and the Tourist Information Office. Cross The Square [057734]
to enter The Pavilion Gardens, and use any variety of paths to reach
the River Wye which flows through the parkland. Follow the river
upstream until Burlington Road is reached [053733]. Across
Burlington Road, The Wye is followed towards the A53, St. John's
Road. The Serpentine Walks cross the river to follow the true right
bank onto the road. Opposite a path below tall trees leads away from
the main road into Gadley Lane.

Take the lane, ford the Wye, follow Gadley Lane between Brick-
yard Plantation and Gadley Plantation until Watford Road comes in
from the right. Here, on the corner of Cavendish Golf Course, follow

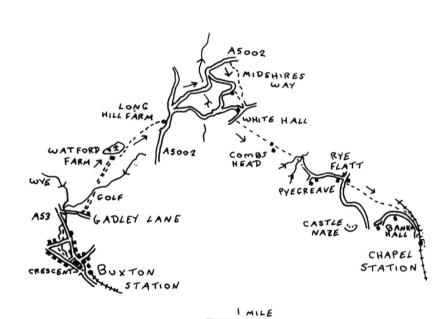

A5002

MIDSHIRES
WAY

LONG
HILL FARM

WHITE HALL

WATFORD
FARM   A5002   COMBS
                                           HEAD   RYE
                                                             FLATT

WYE   PYEGREAVE

GOLF

A53

GADLEY LANE   CASTLE
                                                  NAZE   BANK
                                                                   HALL

CRESCENT   BUXTON   CHAPEL
           STATION   STATION

1 MILE

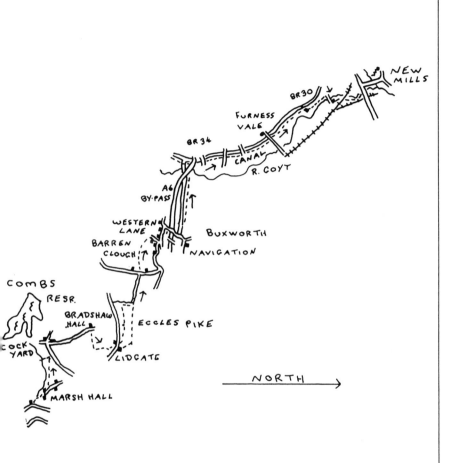

BUXTON TO NEW MILLS

a rough road through the links, heading to distant Watford Farm. Ample signs warn of golf balls, keep to the correct line across the fairways. At the head of the links go through a gate [041741]. The track climbs to the farm and turns north on the edge of Watford Wood.

A track runs level at the foot of the wood. Turning north west and through a gate, the path enters open moorland, aiming to Long Hill Farm.

The route follows a slight depression through reed beds, the A5004 is visible across the valley. Aim for the farm. In the last few hundred yards the route passes a particularly wet hollow. Go through a broken wall to a gate close to the farm yard. The path diverts away from the farm, its route is neither well-marked nor stiled. Once over the gate and the ruined wall on the left, skirt behind a shed on the left and through a gap in the wall on the summit. Keep high and west of the farm [034750] until a fence heads to the A5004, over a stile to a finger-post doubling as a bus stop for Summer services.

Walk onto the summit of Long Hill Road, fourteen hundred feet above sea level. Turn into Goyt's Lane and discover Old Long Hill Road in the angle between the two roads. If time permits, go down Goyt's Lane, passing the rain gauge to view the shrine [029753]. Return to the summit and take the old road, predating the turnpike, through to Rake End, back onto the A5004 [025759]. Go down the main road for a quarter of a mile then, at the Midshires Way marker on the right, leave the road and follow the bridle track which climbs onto the ridge with views across Erwood Reservoir and the Goyt Valley. Through the summit wall, the waymarked path runs east onto a viewpoint high above the Long Hill bends. Finally, follow the wall to White Hall. Walking east, skirt the hall wall and join the route of a Roman road. Derbyshire Education Authority purchased White Hall fifty years ago, intending it to become an outdoor pursuits centre. During the war it had housed evacuees from Guernsey.

White Hall was promoted by Jack Longland, Derbyshire's Director of Education. Following the opening in 1951, warden Peter Mosedale relied on volunteer climbers and walkers to staff the centre. Geoffrey Bridge succeeded Mosedale, and four years later Eric Langmuir took the post before moving to warden Glenmore Lodge in the Cairngorms. Visited by the Duke of Edinburgh in 1958, White Hall established a precedent among outdoor centres that is now widely and successfully imitated.

Passing White Hall drive, turn right up the Roman road. Look for a stile on the left. Peak and Northern Sign 95, dating from 1938, points the way to Chapel en le Frith via Combs. Go over the stile [034763]. This path follows the wall north west, through various wet spots and over a stile. There is then a wall to the left. Go over another stile then descend, following fence and gully, to Combs Head Farm. The high cliffs of Combs Edge and the Combs valley amphitheatre lie to the east. Pass to the west of the farm, down the field below the buildings. In time, keep a wall to the left. When there's a choice of two gateways, take the one on the right, again following walls, to a stile into the Meveril Brook valley. Cross the footbridge. A few yards ahead, go over the second bridge which is a large stone slab. Iron brackets, leaded into the stone, support a handrail. Walk up the field, following a muddy track rising to Allstone Lea onto the farm drive at the sign post erected in the fortieth year of Eccles CHA., 1986 [043776].

Go north along the road, past Dear Leap, down to the farms at Rye Flatt where Herbert Frood first experimented with brake pads before establishing his factory, Ferodo, at Chapel en le Frith. Walk down onto the road, cross Pyegreave Brook and go right towards the mill ruin. Find the sign dedicated to David Bellhouse. Here a flagged path climbs to a wall. Keep the wall to the right until it ends as you walk uphill. When you reach the rolling hilltop, continue going for the highest land until two shallow craters are passed.

There are a gate and stile in the wall on the hill top [048786]. Combs Reservoir lies to the west, Castle Naze to the east. Turning to the north west, the path reaches and climbs a second wall. The path now runs level across the top of steep hillsides, with the railway at its feet. Stay level, skirting fallen trees and gorse bushes, until the path finally follows a power line then slowly descends to the railway, which it follows around to the east. Eventually, a gate is reached and an exit made onto the Bank Hall Lane.

On reaching the lane, a short path cuts off left, back towards the railway through shrubs, and descends steps to pass below the railway [053794]. Having gone below the railway, the walk could end. Following the path beside the railway east, brings the High Peak 60 to Chapel Station for regular daily trains to Manchester, Stockport, New Mills or Buxton.

Alighting from the train at Chapel, go to the crossing gate beside the restaurant then follow the line west. The path edges away from the track and runs to the railway bridge.

Take the road from the railway. At Downlee Farm it crosses a bridge dated 1830. Follow the road to a kissing gate on the left. The path follows fences, crosses two stiles, the second in a pool of water, then negotiates a saturated stretch of land to reach the stile into the yard at Marsh Hall [050799]. Wade into the yard, and follow the track until another stream channels below the lane. At this point go left and over a stile. The path runs down a flat stream valley, reaching a stile onto the golf course. Walk straight down the links, following white posts. The ground to the west rises slowly. Go to a stile. From here follow the hedge of a parcel of rough pasture onto Manchester Road, Cockyard [042800].

Turn towards Tunstead Milton. Opposite The Hanging Gate go north up Bradshaw Lane, passing the new golf club house, rising to reach Bradshaw Hall. This is an old property, note the architecture and on passing the building, look left to discover the heavy stone arch linking the rear yard to the stable blocks. At the end of the drive, go through a stile on the right and follow the fence east, over the stile at the trough and then follow the fence towards Lidgate. Go over another stile then take a diagonal path across the next field. After a stone stile, head north, following the wall to the side of Lidgate for an exit onto Eccles Pike Road.

A sign dating from 1906 gives the altitude as 973 feet. A memorial to Henry Brown, Geologist and Botanist, for 27 years Secretary of Stockport Field Club, was added in July 1939. The sign marks a route from Buxton via Combs which is very much in accord with the line of High Peak 60 [041812]. Turn uphill, and go right onto National Trust land, part of Eccles Pike. Walk close to the roadside fence as you rise up onto the Pike's 1213 feet summit. There is a fine view from here: Kinder is to the north, Combs Edge to the south, and there are views west across the Whaley Moors into Cheshire and Manchester.

From the summit, walk west along the ridge to the wall then north, following the wall, down into the Black Brook Valley. Chinley is below, and Chinley Churn ahead. Follow the wall down to a lane. Walk in a westerly direction to the road at Portobello [029815]. Cross the lane on a poor stile and descend into Barren Clough, aiming slightly south to follow the wall into the clough bottom. Go over the stream to the stile. Climbing and heading north west, the faint path skirts gorse to the power line and reaches a spur above Buxworth. Follow the broken wall to the metal gate and down the road onto Western Lane. On reaching the tarmac, go west again to cross the by-pass and reach The Navigation beside the canal.

From Buxworth [022820] follow the track passing the restored canal basins, soon to have their own feed of water from the Black Brook. In the next few years restoration work on the connecting arm to the Peak Forest Canal will enable narrow boats to sail up to The Navigation. Leaving the basins, the canal narrows at a toll lock where a toll keeper, occupying the adjacent cottage, would have measured a barge's draught and calculated a tonnage based on cargo, prior to levying a toll. After the lock, the Buxworth Branch passes cottages. An overflow weir is visible over the wall shortly before the canal passes below the A6 by-pass.

Still following the towing path, High Peak 60 crosses the Goyt. A horse tunnel passes below the cut. At the footbridge the route joins that of the Goyt Way and Midshires Way [013823]. Returning to New Mills, the walk turns north, following the Peak Forest Canal. It runs below two further by-pass bridges and reaches Bridgemont. At no point is the canal crossed, but the bridges serve as landmarks. Bridge 34 is Botham's Hall Swivel Bridge. Pass under Bridge 33,

Greensdeep, heading into Furness Vale. Bridge 32, Bongs Swivel Bridge, is passed *en route* to 31, Furness Bridge [009836].

Walk through Furness Vale, passing marinas with varieties of narrow boats moored on the offside. At Bridge 30, Carr Swing Bridge, leave the canal and go down to Carr Farm [005842]. From the farm, go through a gate on the left to walk in fields between the canal and river. The track comes to a gate, rejoins the Goyt Way and crosses the Goyt at Goytside.

Pass the farm to a junction of tracks and go left [004846] to the railway viaduct. Pass below the arches and when the track rises, take the path running down the river's true right bank into the Old Mill Leat. This is followed below Queens Road Bridge to the junction of the Sett and the Goyt. The Sett is crossed at Millward Memorial Bridge [001852], dedicated to a local G.P. who campaigned for the Torrs to become the park under the town.

Sixty miles or more have been walked since we left New Mills four days ago. All that's left is to walk through the mill ruins, below Union Road Bridge, and finally up the long flight of steps back to the Heritage Centre and bus station.

The Log of High Peak 60

Friday May 5th, 1995 dawned bright with a forecast of clear skies and high temperatures. A large group of walkers stood around New Mills bus station ready for a nine thirty start. Of those who had vowed to complete all four days, Pauline had arrived on the train from Leeds via Manchester; Kevin and Christine drove in from Preston; Richard and Roger arrived from Glossop, as did Lillian and Ken; and Steve and Colin came on the bus from Marple. A photographer from the "High Peak Echo" was on hand.

The 361 bus came in from Glossop, bringing in another batch of ramblers. After a short welcome and a resume of the first day's walking, the party, some thirty strong, began the descent into The Torrs. The photographer recorded the event. The group went down to the Sett, following a track leading up to the Sett Valley Trail. Within half an hour the Sett Valley Trail was left behind, steps threaded up to Sitch Lane, Thornsett and across the fields to Rowarth. The Little Mill Inn was reached at 11.10 am.

After a meal break, the walkers climbed to the Combs Plateau, trod the lip of Coombes Rocks and descended The Banks into Charlesworth for lunch on the recreation ground at 1.00 pm

Sitting on the mown grass of the sports field, the more observant members of the group noted a botanical phenomenon. The dandelions and daisies grew only in narrow lines, some straight, others curving. After much debate it was agreed that these plants were growing along the markings of a former football pitch. The white lime paint had neutralized the acid soil, enhancing this flora.

It was apparent that the day was warmer than forecast, making fast walking an effort. The group went to Warhurst Fold Bridge and crossed into Tameside, before returning to High Peak over Best Hill

Bridge. By 2.40 pm, the party had reached Melandra Castle. The last bus to New Mills ran at 5.15 pm so it looked as if the route via Blackshaw was out of the question.

Through the industrial landscape of Woolley Bridge, the walkers came to Waterside and then reached Hadfield Station via Brosscroft and Roughfields. Here Pauline departed for Crowden Youth Hostel, and the remainder slogged over the summit of Mouselow. At Hilltop, Roger and Richard left for Simmondley. The remainder descended to Wood's Park and walked down North Road, reaching Glossop for 5.00 pm Several members of the group took the 394 bus to Marple, the survivors boarded the 5.15 pm 361, returning them to New Mills bus station some eight hours after setting off.

Saturday May 6th, 1995. Another hot day was forecast. A dozen walkers caught the 9.15 am bus to Glossop, another dozen awaited them at Norfolk Square, and by ten o' clock the walk was under way, crossing Ellison Street *en route* to Manor Park. On reaching The Queens, Old Glossop, a further seven, including Pauline back from Crowden, joined the party. Sweating beneath a burning sun, the party slogged up Doctor's Gate and crossed Old Woman into the shelter of Lady Brook. Lunch was had at 1.00 pm in the forest shade at Birchen Clough. Several went onto The Snake Inn. Mid afternoon saw the party crossing the Ashop and walking up to Hope Cross. It was imperative for those returning to Glossop that they board the 4.50 pm train to New Mills, enabling them catch the last bus back to Glossop.

At the top of Jaggers Clough, it was decided to go to Edale for the train. In retrospect, everyone had varying degrees of dehydration, but all pressed on down the bridle road to Ladybrook Booth. For once they were glad the train was late, that extra fifteen minutes enabled people to catch the service. Rather than risk missing the 361 at New Mills, the Glossop members stayed on the train to Marple, enabling them to catch the last 394 back into Glossop.

Sunday May 7th, 1995. A cooler day, cloudy with less sun. This day's walking had been integrated into the Rambler's Association programme of Sunday Walks. When they reached Hope on the train departing New Mills at 10.06 am, the 35 walkers split into two groups. Those intent on walking to Buxton began at once, a few minutes later Bob Kellock set off at a slower pace with half the group making for Peak Dale and a return bus to New Mills. The route followed the road to Hope Church then went by Peak's Hole Water to Castleton, reaching Cave Dale for 11.30 am. After climbing through the dale, a chill wind cooled the party as they crossed the moor towards Peak Forest. Whilst lunching close to The Cop, a chill, icy squall swept across the high limestone plateau. Beyond Peak Forest, the dales provided sheltered walking to Wormhill. A late afternoon snack was enjoyed at Well Head Farm. After Flag Dale, Blackwell Mill Cottages on the River Wye were reached at 4.40 pm. Several ramblers walked off onto the A6 for the Buxton bus, ensuring a connection back to Glossop. The remainder ascended to the top of Wye Dale and after descending to cross the Wye, climbed up to King Sterndale. They then followed the Midshires Way back through Staden to Buxton, reaching Buxton Market Ground at 6.15 pm.. Most people rested in pubs close to the railway whilst awaiting the 7.20 pm train.

Monday May 8th, 1995. A cool, windy day with occasional light rain. The journey to Buxton was made on the 901 bus. Running from Huddersfield, the bus called at Glossop and ran via New Mills and Whaley Bridge, reaching Buxton at 11.10 am. The thirty three extra walkers using the double deck bus were perturbed when, at 10.59, the driver pulled off the road on the summit of Long Hill and switched off the engine. All was revealed when the driver addressed the passengers.

It was V.E. Day and, at the request of Yorkshire Traction, we would hold two minutes' silence. Everyone sat there, the only sounds were the wind sighing across the moors and the creak of the bus as it swayed in the breeze. The engine finally coughed into life and the descent was made into Buxton.

The route ran through the Serpentine Walks, up Gadley Lane, across the golf course and into the yards at Watford Farm. A goose hissed and threatened exposed legs. In a second Brian Goddard had plucked a broom off a midden and swept the goose off the track. Facing a cold west wind, the ramblers crossed the summit of Long

Hill and sheltered for lunch on the old turnpike. After walking a section of the Midshires Way at Rake End, the group descended towards Combs, crossed the railway at Chapel Station and reached Marsh Hall. As it was mid-afternoon on a Bank Holiday, the golfers were not amused as a crocodile of hikers, sticking strictly to the line of the right of way, crossed the fairways making for Cockyard.

Several of the party left at the Hanging Gate, awaiting a bus to New Mills. The stalwarts climbed to the summit of Eccles Pike. A victory bonfire had been built and would be lit at dusk. Down through Buxworth and onto the canal. Lengths of the Goyt Way and Midshires Way sped quickly past until we were back beside the Sett.

Here were the steps ascending to the bus station from which the walk began four days earlier. The majority favoured finishing at New Town Station so we walked up to The Rock Tavern, across the canal and onto New Town Station for buses to Marple and Glossop, and trains to Stockport and Manchester.

So ended High Peak 60, four days of fun and friendship. Each day was walked by over twenty ramblers and ten completed all four days. This book is dedicated to these ten.

5

A High Peak Extension

The selected route for High Peak 60 was never intended to be a High Peak boundary walk, to the north and east large areas of remote moorland are left unvisited. For those competent in navigating through the wilderness and suitably equipped, there is an option of extending the route. This option could involve an overnight stay at Crowden, either on the camp site or in the Youth Hostel, alternatively an express bus linking Manchester to Sheffield, via the A628, can be caught to or from Crowden.

To extend the High Peak 60, the first day's walk would run from New Mills to Crowden. The second day would be from Crowden to Fairholmes (13 miles), where buses can be caught on Summer Sundays and Bank Holiday Mondays, or from Fairholmes 3 miles further to the Ladybower Inn for an infrequent bus each day to Sheffield or Castleton. Four miles further from Fairholmes, Edale Youth Hostel can be reached, or it is five miles to Hope for the train home. Whichever option is selected, an eighteen mile hike can be anticipated for the second day.

Reaching Crowden is easy. When the first day's walk reaches Valehouse Reservoir [031974], a concessionary bridle way runs north of Valehouse Reservoir up to the embankment of Rhodeswood Dam [043981]. The bridle way continues up to Torside Dam [056985] where the Pennine Way is met and followed along the Torside Trail through a strip of pine woodland. When the Pennine Way rises to the A628 road, take the path descending towards the reservoir shore. This path crosses the bywash then runs close to the water's edge. Cross the junction of Crowden Brook with Torside Reservoir. The path turns onto the A628 opposite the old Crowden

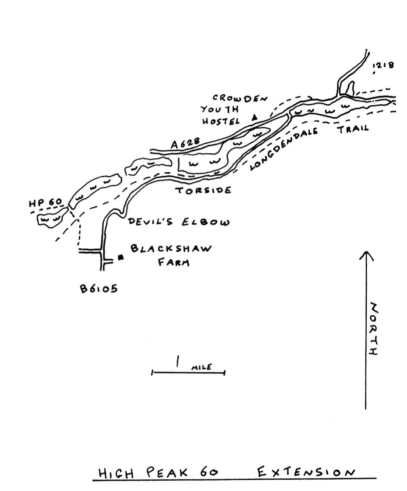

HIGH PEAK 60   EXTENSION

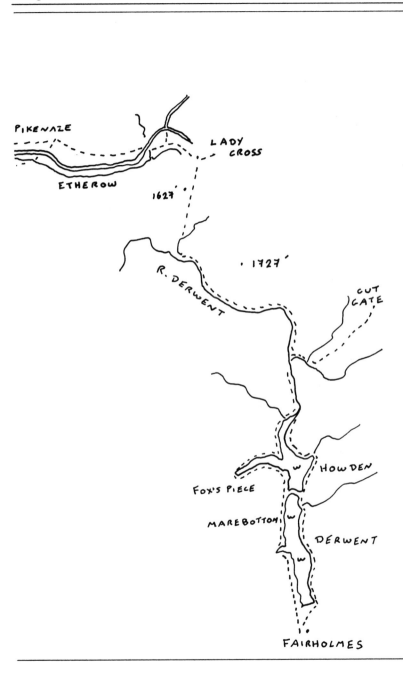

PIKENAZE

LADY CROSS

ETHEROW

1627

R. DERWENT

1727

CUT GATE

HOWDEN

FOX'S PIECE

MAREBOTTOM

DERWENT

FAIRHOLMES

School. The coach stop is a little to the west, the Youth Hostel at Stone Row lies a few minutes along the road to the north east.

Setting out from Crowden, follow the A628 towards Woodhead. The road is heading to Bleak House, perched above Woodhead Dam. On the left a track rises up to St. James's Church [080995]. This track is followed past the church and burial yard. Go through the gate and follow the path, which was once the salter's road through Longdendale. This path descends back to the A628 at Hey Clough. Walk east, facing the traffic, to the A6024 junction where The George and Dragon Inn once stood[091998]. Keep with the A628, cross Nine Arches Bridge then turn left towards Pikenaze Farm. Take another section of the salt road heading east, rising towards the top of Woodhead Tunnel. Out into open country the track reaches Audernshaw Clough [115002]. Here a section of Trans Pennine Trail is being constructed which will lead down to the Longdendale Trail at the tunnel mouth.

The road crosses Ironbower Moss to Longside and re-crosses the A628, reaching the infant Etherow at Salterbrook [137999]. Cross the river on the restored bridge, leaving High Peak for South Yorkshire. Staying with the old road, walk past farm ruins onto Lady Shaw Moss. These were once thriving hamlets servicing the turnpike traffic over the Pennines. At fifteen hundred feet the watershed between the Etherow and the Don, the Irish Sea and the North Sea is reached [148997]. From here it is necessary to walk on a bearing of 214 degrees across Round Hill to Dean Head Stones [140981] and to the infant Derwent. The river, the county boundary, is followed downstream for three miles to a path on the true left bank to Cranberry Clough [170953] where the Cut Gate path crosses the river. Keep to the eastern side of Howden Reservoir, part of the Cal-Der-Went Walk, below Cold Side Oaks to Howden Dam. Finally, go down the length of Derwent Reservoir to Derwent Dam [174899]. Here descend steps onto the valley floor to reach Fairholmes Information Centre [172893], from where various choices of route to Edale or Hope are available.

6

Glossop Go Round

Five miles around Glossop

Glossop is served by trains from Manchester six days a week. Frequent buses run to Manchester, either through Hyde or Ashton. Daily buses run to Stockport via Hayfield and New Mills. Monday to Saturday a service links with Charlesworth and Marple to Hazel Grove. Summer services run to Huddersfield, Castleton and Buxton.

Dark Peak map required.

Carry a pair of secateurs. Walk on lanes and farmland paths. Some wet spots are met on this circuit of Glossop.

From the traffic lights in the centre of Glossop, go east along High Street east, looking on the right for Milltown [038941]. Reaching Milltown go down the street, passing the Kingdom Hall and The Prince of Wales. The road runs between the high walls of Howard Town Mill and onto the bridge over Shelf Brook. Cross the bridge, turn upstream to the junction of Hurst Clough with the Shelf, a spot called Scotland Brook. From here a passage leaves the stream, runs between new houses, crosses the estate road and rises up steps to the terrace of older houses at Cross Cliffe [040939].

Go right, passing the gable end, opposite a sign and stile. Here a steep field path climbs, following the fence. At the top of the slope go left and then right, following the path onto the hill top. At the stile examine the rounded stone stump, possibly a remnant of Whitfield Cross. From here the path crosses narrow strip fields and

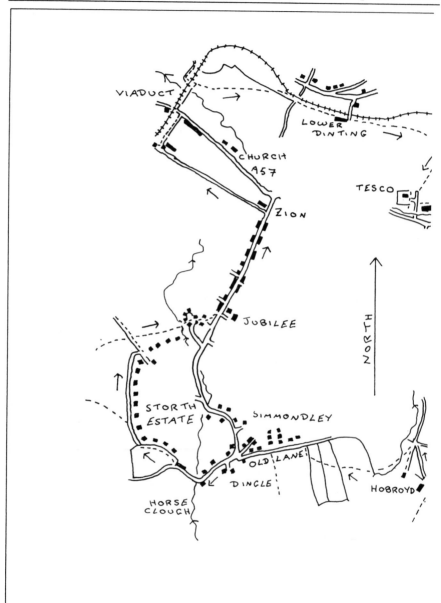

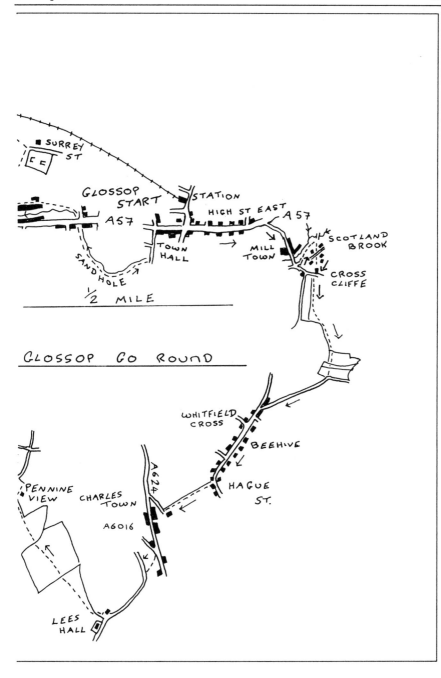

good stone stiles until a narrow lane is met [040935]. Take the lane uphill. Looking back, the view reaches to Dowstone Clough draining off Bleaklow and views ahead open out across Whitfield and Charlestown to Whitley Nab and Hobroyd.

This lane runs towards Cliffe Road, within fifty yards of the houses a stone on the right marks the way to Glossop. On reaching the road, examine the terrace on the right accredited to Joel Bennet. Walk left, passing Padfield Gate, to Whitfield Cross. Note the date on the house on the left after The Beehive. Look right for the V.R. mail box and discover Hague's School. Read the plaque on the wall and see the beehive carved above the door [037933].

Joseph Hague was born on Chunal in 1695. Earning money as a pedlar, he reached London at the age of 21 and entered the cotton trade. After making his fortune he retired to Derbyshire, settling at Park Hall, Hayfield. Mindful of the poor of his native parish, he had the Hague Street School built and endowed the Hague Trust, still surviving today.

Proceed along Hague Street. There are several old properties, one with an early seventeenth century datestone. As the street turns, look on the left for Flagged Field Barn opposite house number 61. Spot the rabbit on the flying buttress of the barn. Go right immediately before the barn, down the front of the cottages, through a stile and past a discreet footpath sign. The path descends a passage, secateurs ready!

At the bottom of this wild path a house drive is joined and followed right. Emerging from behind the mill onto Charlestown [033931], go left on the A624 road. Between the mills, glimpses of Bray Clough can be seen. On the corner of Chunal and Turnlee Road stands The Drovers. Cross Turnlee Road then, opposite The Whiteley Nab go up the bank and follow a flagged path, secateurs ready! Reaching the rough road, follow it into Long Clough and up to Lees Hall Farm. On reaching Lees Hall [032926], go through the gate on the right and after following the wall, go over a stile. Aim across the field towards distant Dinting Arches. The path bears north west through fields to Hobroyd.

After crossing three fields, it descends, crossing a flood ditch, to a converted barn and reaches Pennine View, the extended nursing home built on the site of Levi Jackson's Hobroyd Ropeworks.

Passing the front of Pennine View, a narrow passage is trod between high hedges [028932]. Using secateurs, clip off a few twigs, making the route easier for the next walker. At the end of the passage go through a stile and cross the drive to Hobroyd Farm. Over the drive, the walk goes to a stream which flows down the path. Go through the stile and up the field. After the stile below the trees, the path crosses wet land to a stile in a holly bush. After a further stone stile with an inadequate wall, go down into Old Lane, at the rear of Simmondley [024932].

The lane runs behind High View, when the properties of The Croft and Spinney Cottage are seen. Take a detour down the cul-de-sac on the right, with a view of the restored farms, barns and cottages comprising Simmondley Village. Return to Old Lane and walk forward to The Hare and Hounds, dated 1784. Proceed along High Lane into Horse Clough, the school on the right is dated 1844. Walk past Storth Brook Farm and up Storth Brow. After the cottages on the right, a sign post takes the walk into the field [019932]. Follow the wall, skirting the gardens of Storth Bank estate. The path crosses the wall and runs in a passage between gardens and a field fence to Green Lane. Secateurs are useful here.

Reaching Green Lane go left, away from the houses, then right where a path [017936] cuts across building sites into a stream valley. A path is being surfaced. After crossing the brook and entering the estate between houses 7 & 9, the path leaves between houses 14 & 16, reaching Simmondley Lane opposite The Jubilee and Pennine Road.

Turn down Simmondley Lane [021939] towards Dinting Vale, A57. Above Zion Methodist Chapel, take the track, which is cobbled in the early stages and runs towards the railway and Adderley Place. Below the railway embankment, go into a garden where steps, often slippery, descend to Adderley Road. Between the chip shop and the viaduct, cross the A57 [019944].

From the foot of the railway bridge, take the path passing the piers. After crossing Glossop Brook through a right-hand stile, follow the path up to Dinting Lane. It emerges at the site of the former Dinting Railway Museum. In the history of the museum, footplate rides on "Bahamas", "Flying Scotsman", "Blue Peter" and "Scots Guardsman" have been enjoyed. Out of the gateway onto Dinting Lane, one can take the road from the level crossing, [023945] walking beside the line to Lower Dinting. For a *soupcon* more of Glossop's history, cross the railway, go up onto Dinting Road and look in the garden of the former Vicarage at Higher Dinting. Here is a memorial to Nicholas Garlick, born Dinting 1555, ordained a priest 1582, arrested at Padley when a threatened Spanish Armada excited anti-Catholic feelings and executed at Derby on July 24th 1588.

From Higher Dinting go east along Dinting Road, descend to Lower Dinting. On crossing the railway bridge, turn left. A wet track, soon to be diverted around industrial units, leads to the corner of Glossop's football ground at Surrey Street [028943]. Here take the path towards Tesco, onto Glossop Brook Road. Go towards the A57. Turn left through the rear of Wren Nest Mill, passing between the buildings to the brick chimney with date stone and onto Shrewsbury Street at its junction with High Street West [031941].

Return to the town centre by crossing High Street West. Follow the stream through the Sandhole. This leads to Market Street. A left turn past the market ground leads back to Norfolk Square in the centre of Glossop.

7

New Mills Circuit

A seven-mile circuit around New Mills

New Mills has two rail links into Manchester. One, via Marple, reaches Central Station *en route* to Sheffield. The Buxton to Stockport and Manchester railway uses Newtown Station. Allow fifteen minutes to walk via Albion Road and Union Road to reach the Heritage Centre. In the town centre there is a bus station serviced from Whaley Bridge, Macclesfield, Glossop, Marple, Stockport and Hayfield. This six mile circuit begins at the bus station and passes Central Station. The walk can commence at either place.

Dark Peak map and Pathfinder 741 required.

Tracks and field paths. One ascent early in the walk.

Head west from the bus station onto the B6101. Turn down Station Road and pass Central Station [998853]. The gradient eases as the road reaches the River Goyt. There are Goyt Way and Midshires Way signs. Follow the road to Mousley Bottom, passing the site of the gas works. After the scrap yard on the left, ignore the track between the stone and brick houses and continue to a dilapidated cruck barn with flag stone roof. Go through the gate with the Midshires Way sign. Behind the barn, a surfaced track crosses the site of a refuse tip. The alder, birch and willow herb are growing well, keep with the path through the undergrowth. Cross a track, go over the high stile beside the gate and reach the Goyt.

The footpath runs beside the river, meandering through shrubs to

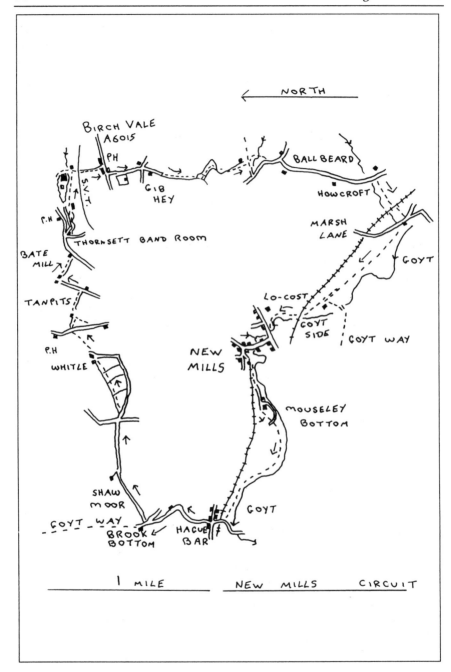

the Midshires Way stump unveiled by Benny Rothman on June 21st. 1994 [991851]. It's 15 miles to the Trans Pennine Trail at Stockport or 220 miles to the Ridgeway in Buckinghamshire. Keep to the river bank, and when the bushes are left behind, go onto flat grazing land. After crossing the fence stretching across the meadow, take the sandy path uphill to the wooded slopes of the railway embankment. Walk to the car park and recreation ground at Waterside Road.

A flight of steps leads onto the railway bridge. Cross the line onto the B6106 at Hague Bar [986857]. Across the road stands Toll Bar Cottage. Take Hague Fold Road as it climbs to Lower Hague Fold. Still with the Goyt Way and Midshires Way, keep climbing to Higher Hague Fold where there is a well in the wall foundation. The tarmac ends and the surface becomes sandy. Pause to take in the view.

Looking from south to west the views reach Sponds Hill, Lyme Cage and Jackson Edge. The lower Goyt valley is girded by Marple Ridge. Industry is evident in the shape of Bowater's Drum Factory beside the canal at Disley, the paper mill down by the river and the chimney of the textile mills at Strines.

Walk the rough road onto Brook Bottom Road [987862]. Take the stony track opposite, noting the wall stone indicating Clough Bank Farm. This track, partly cut into bed-rock, rises onto Shaw Marsh, with a golf course to one side and the county boundary on the other. In time the rough road levels and ahead are views to Kinder Scout [991865].

After Shaw Farm the surface improves *en route* to the club house at the junction of Apple Tree Road and Eaves Knoll Road. Go down Apple Tree Road, to a finger post on the left. Go over the stile and follow the wall on the left, crossing three stiles to Whitle [999867]. A finger post stands in the centre of this hamlet. Go onto Whitle Bank Road and through the stile by the bridle way sign.

Descend to Mellor Road close to the Pack Horse Inn [001869]. Cross Mellor Road and through the red gate a path descends to red-painted Tanpits. Pass the farm and go below the lower barns to a stile by the power line pole. Turn left to the stone stile in the corner, climb over this and go down the field to Watford Lane [005867]. On reaching the lane, turn north below the power lines to Sunnnyside Farm at Cobsters.

On reaching the first house with a large glass conservatory, leave the track, go through a stile on the right and down to a lower field. Follow the field wall on the right to an iron kissing gate at Bate Mill and exit onto Bate Mill Road. Walk to Thornsett Band Institute, 1932, on the corner of High Hill Road and Bate Mill Road [009869].

Enter Thornsett Trading Estate and follow the road over the Sett to the mills. Cross a drain on the right to Hypo Engineering and head east past a fishing pond. An overgrown path runs through shrubs to the Sett Valley Trail at Wilde's Crossing [014867].

This walk can be shortened by following the Trail back into New Mills.

From Wilde's Crossing a cobbled lane leads onto Hayfield Road, A6015, at The Vine. Cross the road and pass Birch Vale's terraced cricket field to a track junction at Gibb Hey [015862]. Go left and first right to Higher Gibb Hey. Pass a farm and buildings, go through a gate and along the fence and hedge, following the pylon line to a stile. Here is Peak and Northern signpost 229, erected 1992, in memory of Glenda of Whitle. Go onto the track, reach a pylon on a shale heap [014857] and go through a stile in the fence. Follow the power line to a gateway. Beyond here the path hugs the wall, crosses the wall and continues to the ruined Pingot Cottage. From the cottage go south across the spoil heaps to a solitary oak, cross the brook and follow a trench to a stile and sign on Laneside Road [015851].

Ascend the lane to the barn and turn right. Ignore the fork to Ballbeard Farm, and descend with the bridle road, passing Butterbank Plantation and Howcroft Farm to Shedyard Clough. Go across the clough to a stile on the right. From here a path runs to the railway [013841] and tunnels below the line to reach Lady Pit Road.

Join the road and go to the junction with Marsh Lane. After passing the farm on the left, enter the field and walk a wide track through the fields to the Goyt Way at Goytside Farm [004846].

By Goytside the surface improves. Continue down the valley,

below the railway viaduct and beside the river. A path on the left leads to the Old Mill Leat, and after passing below Queen's Bridge, crosses the Millward Memorial Bridge on the confluence of the Sett and the Goyt. Walk down river to the foaming weir, and through the mill ruins inside The Torrs Park. Do not cross the river, go below Union Road Bridge and, after the climbing crag, ascend the long run of steps up to the Heritage Centre.

Visit the Centre for refreshments, guide books and local history displays, finally reaching the bus station which is just around the corner.

8

Phoside Foray

A five-mile circuit of Hayfield

Hayfield can be reached by regular daily buses from Stockport, New
Mills and Marple. There is also a regular service from Glossop, less
frequent on Sunday. On Summer Sundays and Bank Holiday Mondays buses connect to Huddersfield, Chesterfield, Buxton and Macclesfield.

Dark Peak map required.

Some ascents. Field paths and one steep descent.

From Hayfield bus station with its car park, toilets and Information
Office, take Station Road away from the site of Hayfield Station,
which closed on December 31st. 1969. On reaching New Mills Road,
A6015, cross and enter Chapel Street. The road climbs, passing
Meadows Farm and Ridge Top Cottage. Finally, the track rises and
turns right. Up on the bank is a sign post, scramble up to it [034865].

This is Peak and Northern signpost 216, showing the way to Peep
O'Day via Phoside. Erected in 1989, the sign is a memorial to a
former member of New Mills Group of the RA, Sid Needham, who
died August 1987, aged 65. Throughout this walk several Peak and
Northern signs will be met. At the end of the walk look on the wall
of the Hayfield Information Office to view a centenary plaque
unveiled by the Peak and Northern in August 1994.

From the sign take a footpath running south east, following the
eight hundred foot contour to Phoside Farm. Shortly before Phoside

another footpath sign is reached. Go over the stile, walk below trees and pass the large house, dated 1784. [037860] The right of way keeps right of the stable block before descending to the mill ruins in Foxholes Clough. Phoside Mill was in use in the early 1800s for yarn spinning, cloth dressing and weaving. The water-wheel was removed in the 1920s.

Pass the mill ruin and cross the stream. The walk heads out into the fields and continues south east to pass Far Phoside [041857].

The path, classified as a bridle road, continues to head south east towards Hills House. Rising gradually to cross the thousand-foot contour, the ground can be wet, one section of path has had its surface improved. The track reaches Mainstone Road close to Chapel Road, and turns to pass Hills House to join the A624 at Peep O'Day. Signpost 215, in memory of James Williams, stands at the end of the bridle path [048850].

Hills House has an eye-shaped window above its eastern door. The stone around the window, dating from 1841, bears the names of James and Mary Goddard. This window sees the first peep of daylight, hence the name for the road's summit. On the road side is Peak and Northern signpost 23, dating from 1906 and having an altitude of 1085 feet.

Turn down Chapel Road for a hundred yards, then turn right onto a rough road, rising to pass a shallow quarry where stone is re-worked. Without inciting the reader to trespass, take my word for it, one stone stab in the quarry originates from the grave of:
John Manley of Newton
Who departed this life,
Jan 24th. 1838 in the 28th year of his life.
In a coal pit I lost my life at Bayley Field near Hyde.
To fetch a man out of the damp but woe did me betide.
For both of us did lose our lives upon that fatal day,
so miners all a warning take from this catastrophe.
I think this stone would be better kept in a Tameside Museum than residing in a Hayfield quarry.

Continue along the track until a bridle road running north-south is met [050853]. Across the way there is another sign. This sign

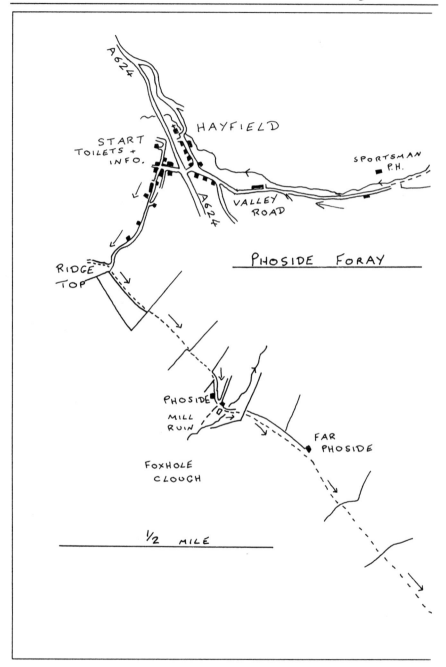

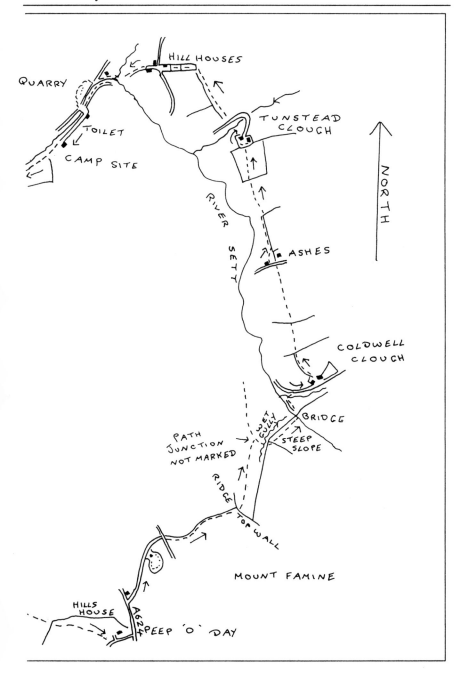

shows the variety of routes crossing at this point: tracks run to Castleton via Roych and Winnats, while other routes head into the Kinder Valley and onto Edale and Woodlands. Our walk leaves the track and follows the bridle path east, rising to the wall in the col at the foot of Mount Famine. Pass through the gate and commence a descent into the Sett Valley. Views ahead leap onto Kinder Low End and into Oaken Clough.

The path goes downhill, heading north east. To the right of the path, a gully develops at an unmarked path junction, where a solitary rock sits beside a bend in the path [054856]. Go east into the gully and cross the marshy stream margins. Turn down stream and, following the gully's right bank, locate and cross a stile in a fence. Below this point carefully descend a very steep hillside, descend on grass for over a hundred feet to reach the River Sett. Turn down-stream and discover a footbridge [056857].

Cross the Sett and look upstream to admire the bulk of Mount Famine rising from the river, then take the path downstream. Leaving the Sett, and turning to cross a side stream, join the road downhill of Coldwell Clough Farm. Go to Coldwell Clough Farm. Look at the architecture and the date stone before going through a gate on the left, between barn and house, to enter the farm yard. Leave through a second gate, from where a path follows hedges and fences north to Ashes Farm, finally crossing open meadows to reach the drive at The Ashes [055863].

Turn down the drive, looking on the right for a stile. Take the path which cuts below the farm, finally rising to follow re-planted hedge-rows *en route* to Tunstead Clough Farm. Aim directly towards the farm buildings as you cross the open pastures, go through a gate and onto a track [054867]. This track is followed down and around the buildings until Tunstead Clough is crossed. After the culvert, follow the lane downhill, and look left for a stile up the bank. Having met this stile, go into fields and follow wall foundations towards Hill Houses. The path does not aim for the farm, but, going slightly north west, the walk runs to a series of narrow pens east of the farm [053870]. Descend through the pens, taking care if sheep are enclosed within them.

On reaching the road between the farm buildings, pass in front of the main house with date stone, and go into a yard on the right where a barn has been renovated into a dwelling. Opposite the expansive window, pass through a gate to the right and descend a rocky path to a lower gate [050870]. Turn right, following the Sett downstream to its junction with the Kinder, and cross the latter at Bowden Bridge.

Join the road, go to the quarry and locate the plaque telling that here, on April 24th 1932, the Mass Trespass to Kinder Scout began. The moorlands of the High Peak were private, walkers had to obtain permits from the landowner. Many ramblers wanted open access to the moors, so rallies were held, and at Hayfield a more militant group organised the Mass Trespass. After an address by Benny Rothman, the walkers trekked off along the William Clough path. At a predetermined point they left the path and stormed up onto Kinder Scout. Keepers tried to turn them back, but they reached the hill tops. On returning to the valley, the leaders were identified and arrested.

They were detained at New Mills, prior to being held at Derby. Following a trial before a jury better suited to a court martial, Rothman and five others were imprisoned for six months. The plaque in Bowden Bridge Quarry was unveiled on the fiftieth anniversary of the Trespass. It was a post-war Labour Government which drafted the National Parks and Access to Countryside Act. From this Act sprang the National Parks of England and Wales. The Peak District was the first, and within this Act was the legislation which identified the Definitive Rights of Way.

Re-cross the Sett. Pass the toilet block [048869] and walk beside the river, down past the camp site into Valley Road. This is followed through to the centre of Hayfield. Discover The George Hotel, a passage to the rear of the pub shows where Hayfield {Kinder} Mountain Rescue Team keeps its equipment. Here a subway below the by-pass leads back to toilets, car park and bus stop.

9

Edale and the Ridge

Seven miles around Edale

Edale has daily train connections to Manchester and Sheffield. Trains
stop at Marple, New Mills, Chinley and local halts through the Hope
Valley. A few trains run from Manchester, via Stockport. Summer
buses connect the village to Castleton.

Dark Peak map required.

Farmland paths and tracks. After a steep ascent an exposed ridge is
followed. Following the route is not difficult on the high ground.

From Edale railway station [123853], proceed to the road and head
south, passing toilets and car park, to a junction with the road
running roughly east-west down the floor of the Vale of Edale.

Turn west towards Barber Booth, looking on the right for a track
descending to the River Noe. This track is signposted as being a
bridle road to Castleton and is the approach to National Trust
property at Harden Clough. The river is bridged at 770 feet above
sea level, and an eight hundred foot ascent to reach Mam Nick
follows. The total climb, to the summit of Mam Tor, is 925 feet. The
wide track rises slowly through the fields as it passes Harden Clough
Farm [124848] then enters the stream valley. At 900 feet above sea
level, the track turns sharp left to cross the culvert, after which it
rises up through trees before turning south to Greenlands. At this
property the bridle road goes through a gate on the left [125844].
Ignore the sign pointing to Hollins Cross, and keep with the track

climbing to the thousand-feet contour and into the land slips at Cold Side. A T.V. mast is perched on a hillock above the bridle road.

Plantations of trees have become established, one was planted by Edale School. Views are extensive, sweeping from the head of the valley above Jacob's Ladder down to Edale End. The rim of Kinder is visible and the high points of Grindslow Knoll, Broadlee Bank Tor, The Nab and Ringing Roger can usually be identified. Go through a gate, still following the track, which was once an ancient hollow way, and up to Mam Nick. The path is within a gully, swept clean by floods, showing the shale rocks. Finally, the gradient eases, and the tarmac road at Mam Nick is met [125835] and followed through the shale cutting separating Mam Tor from Rushup Edge, out of Edale into Castleton parish. Walk forward, leaving behind vistas over the Dark Peak. Ahead are views across the White Peak.

Once through the cutting, well-constructed steps laid by National Trust estate workers leave the road and commence the climb to the summit of Mam Tor at 1695 feet above sea level [128836]. The climb passes through the ditch system protecting this iron age hill fort and up to the trig point OSBM. S4230. The summit is protected from erosion by stones embedded into the summit dome.

From the top, the breadth of the ridge, stretching from Lord's Seat to Lose Hill, can be absorbed. On warm days thermals attract hang glider pilots and parachutists who sail away off the ridge top. Don't stray too far south beware of the massive shale cliff. The walk descends from the summit on a flagged path heading to Hollins Cross. There is a col on the ridge, and early tracks from Castleton and Edale rise to cross the ridge at this low point.

Hollins Cross [136845], a little below the thirteen hundred foot contour, is marked by a stone pillar, erected in 1964 in memory of Tom Hyett of Long Eaton. An unsurfaced path, showing the wear and tear of many feet, follows the wall on the divide between Edale and Castleton.

The ridge rises onto Barker Bank then drops into Backtor Nook. Ahead is the shale face of Back Tor. The path comes to a stile in the top corner of Brocket Booth Plantation, climb over the fence on the

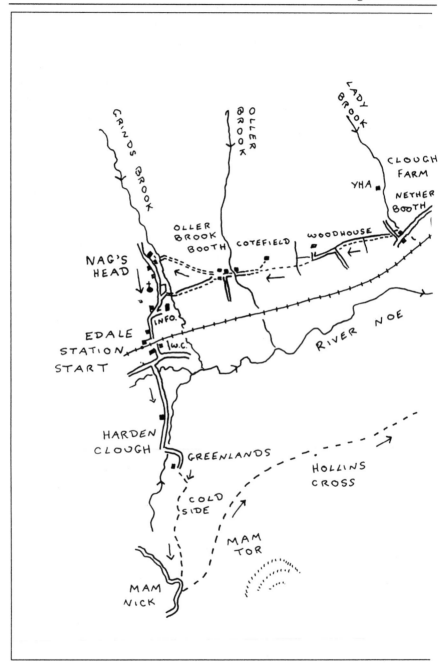

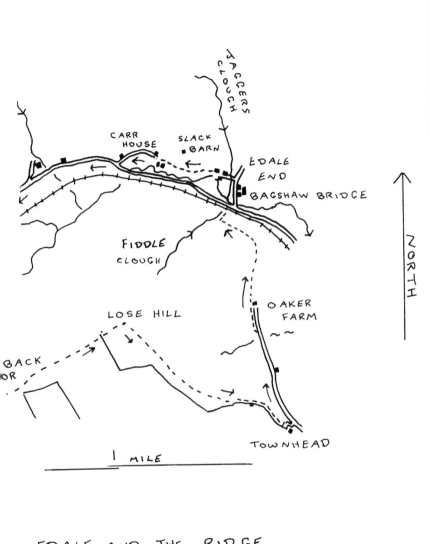

EDALE AND THE RIDGE

left, and ascend Back Tor [145850]. The easiest route is the path climbing close to the fence. From the summit look down over Backtor Wood and Backtor Farm to Nether Booth, and above the Youth Hostel at Rowland Cote onto Upper and Nether Moor.

Follow the wall from Back Tor to the National Trust sign before ascending Lose Hill Pike [153853]. Rest on the peak at 1563 feet. Path restoration has necessitated a massive airlift of flag stones onto this summit. The hill top is also called Ward's Piece after G.H.B. Ward, an early member of the Sheffield Clarion Ramblers, one of the founders of the Peak Branch of the Council for the Preservation of Rural England and organiser of the mass trespasses from Sheffield. The summit view finder was erected in his memory.

A steep descent down a restored path leads to Losehill End. The route follows a wide, windswept, grass spur with views over Hope village. Climb two stiles, the lower one beside a derelict barn, then proceed into a sunken lane and below trees to Townhead Farm [165846]. Reach the tarmac road, 610 feet above sea level, and the lowest point on the walk! Follow it north towards the guest house, Moorgate. The first property on the right, Underleigh, was built by one George Eyre in 1873. Moorgate is an outdoor centre offering guided walks and activity holidays in the Peak District.

Passing Moorgate, the track surface deteriorates. Continue north to Oaker Farm. Shortly before the farm, a path turns off left and passes Oaker to the base of Oaker Tor. After a wet section, go through a gate from where a wide green path rises slightly and turns west. At this point, pause [163859]. Look back over Hope then look ahead into the valley of Jaggers Clough and finally up the Vale of Edale.

The path comes to Fiddle Clough where you should go over a stile, pass below the railway and cross the road. Go down a short path to Bagshaw Bridge, which crosses the Noe close to its confluence with Jaggers Clough. A jagger being a man in charge of a train of pack ponies. Go over the river and up the lane to Edale End [161864]. The farm to the right is a National Trust property, and there is an information shelter, useful for lunch on a cold or wet day. The shelter walls are decorated with information panels about upland farming, ecology and conservation.

Pass the buildings on the right, turn left to cross the clough, and out of Hope into Edale. Go past the farm house. Walk through the yards, the final ones may be gated to enclose cattle. Continue to the ladder stile, out into the field and onto the river bank. Walk upstream beside the meandering Noe until a rough road is met. Follow this towards Carr House, Slack Barn stands up the slope to the north. Approaching Carr House Farm, obvious signs divert the path around the buildings. A well-surfaced drive is followed out onto the main road [152865].

When the road is reached, look left for an iron plate marked M.R., identifying land once owned by the Midland Railway. The Dore and Chinley Railway was opened for goods traffic in 1893, passenger trains first ran on June 25th. 1894. Along the line are two tunnels, Totley and Cowburn. Whilst the latter tunnel was under construction, it was necessary for a locomotive to reach Edale. To achieve this, engineers took an engine off the rails at Chapel en le Frith, and by leap frogging lengths of rail in front of the locomotive they were able to steam it over Rushup Edge, through Mam Nick and down into Edale.

The road is followed for three quarters of a mile. Walk on the right, facing the oncoming traffic. Look across the railway and study the slopes of the ridge between Back Tor and Lose Hill, descending to the valley floor.

Follow the road past a barn, then into a stream valley housing Clough Farm. On the right, pass a Peak and Northern sign 14, dated 1905, marking the start of a bridle road to Alport, Ashopton, Derwent, Snake Inn and Glossop. This route runs via Jaggers Clough to Hope Cross, then as now walkers were reminded to close all gates.

The road passes an Edale sign, crosses Lady Booth Brook [142861] and enters Nether Booth. By Lady Booth Hall on the right, a finger post points to Edale. Take this path, cross the drive to Rowland Cote Youth hostel then follow hedges to the drive of Woodhouse Farm [136860]. The drive is walked until the path exits and crosses a damp patch before becoming better surfaced *en route* to Cotefield. After Cotefield, the track leads into Ollerbrook Clough, crosses Oller Brook and comes to the farms at Ollerbrook Booth [129859].

Pass through the farms and note a G.R. mail box on the bend. Here take the waymarked path into the farm yard on the right, and on into pasture land, walking a wide track. The track heads towards Grinds Brook, approaching the houses in Grindsbrook Booth. A sign on the left directs the walk into the clough, which is crossed on a narrow pack horse bridge. Over the stream, turn right, proceed upstream, and exit left into the yard at The Nag's Head [123860].

Good Friday, April 14, 1954 saw the launch of the National Park Warden Service under the leadership of Britain's first full time warden, Tom Tomlinson. The event was inaugurated by Alderman Charles White at a ceremony outside The Nag's Head.

Here the Pennine Way has its start or finish. Turn down the road, passing the village school. Go down to the Church of the Holy and Undivided Trinity, built in 1887 from rock quarried at Nether Tor. The burial yard opposite, complete with font, has some horizontal memorials, possibly from an earlier church. A little lower down the road is Church Cottage with a date stone of 1678 in the garden wall.

Around the curve, take time to visit the information centre at Fieldhead. Finally continue down the road to the railway, a useful cafe lies beyond the railway bridge, close to the car park and toilets.

10

Edale to Fairholmes

Four miles linking the Noe to the Derwent

Dark Peak map required.
Field paths and well-trodden bridle paths are used.

From Edale Station [123853], go onto Station Road and north towards Grindsbrook Booth. The road bears right, passing Champion House and Fieldhead, the National Park Information Centre – obtain the latest mountain weather forecast here. After Fieldhead, and before the burial yard, a track on the right descends to cross Grinds Brook and runs through fields to Ollerbrook Booth. The track passes the farms. Go across Oller Brook and into Nether Ollerbrook.

At Cotefield the track forks. Heading east, the surfaced path runs into a wet hollow before joining the Woodhouse Farm drive. Walk along the drive for a short distance, go over a stile and follow the fence towards Nether Booth, crossing the drive of Rowland Cote, Edale Youth Hostel. Join the road at Lady Booth Hall Farm. Along the road cross Lady Brook, on the left is a Peak and Northern sign. The sign, dated 1905, points to Ashopton, and walkers are reminded to shut all gates [145864].

Leave the road, follow the track behind Clough Farm, ford the stream and rise to the access point below Nether Moor. Rise onto the ridge between Jaggers Clough and The Noe [154871]. Over the crest, the view stretches over the flank of Crookstone Hill to Crookstone Out Moor. A well-surfaced descent leads to the stream, and

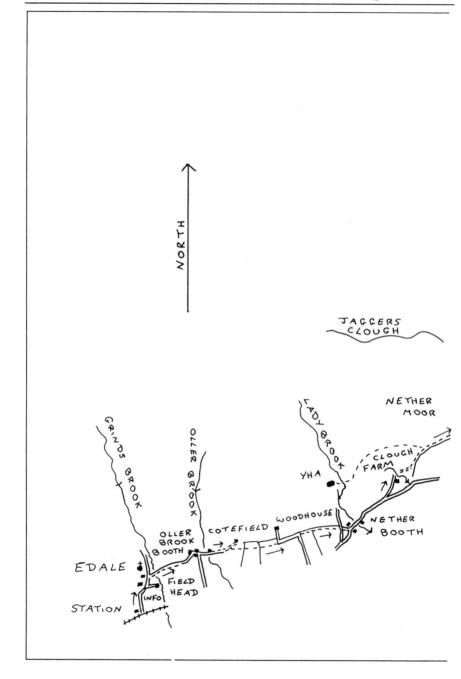

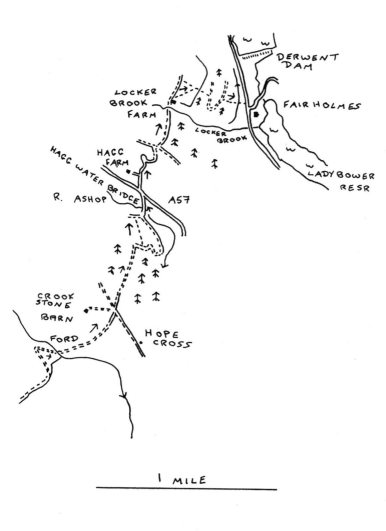

DERWENT DAM

FAIRHOLMES

LOCKER BROOK FARM

LOCKER BROOK

LADYBOWER RESR

HAGG WATER BRIDGE

HAGG FARM

R. ASHOP

A57

CROOK STONE BARN

FORD

HOPE CROSS

1 MILE

EDALE TO FAIRHOLMES

turning to face down the valley, the road runs through the gate and across the ford. Over the brook a rougher track climbs towards Crookstone Barn and reaches the track linking Ashop to Hope. Hope Cross stands a little distance from the track junction.

Across the junction, the rough road enters the forest. Go through the gate into the dark plantation. The bridle road descends and turns a bend [161882] where conifers have been cleared to enable deciduous woodland to become established. A steep path on the left runs north, downhill, direct to Haggwater Bridge. Cross the River Ashop, and a rough road climbs through the wood to join the A57.

Cross the A57, Snake Road, and go up the drive of Hagg Farm, once a Youth Hostel jointly owned by the Peak Park and the YHA. Over twenty years ago, I often brought groups of young people from Glossop to spend the night here. Now it is used by an Education Authority. Pass the entrance to the hostel site and continue, with the road climbing steeply up through the woods onto the ridge between Open Hagg and Hagg Side, the escarpment dividing the Derwent from the Ashop [164890]. On the ridge, go north along the forest fence, with open moorland to the west, and glimpses of the distant Derwent Edges to the east. Lockerbrook Farm approaches. Through clearings in the timber there are superb views down onto Ladybower Reservoir. Sometimes it is possible to get a brew at the Lockerbrook Outdoor Centre. Thirty to fifty yards after the farm, climb a stile over the fence to the right [165895]. From here cross grass land to the top of the forest. Enter the dark woods and walk downhill to a wall. Bearing right, south towards Locker Brook, the path runs down to a logging road. Go down the road, and around the bend discover Forest Enterprises signs indicating the line of this concessionary path to Fairholmes. The path runs to a concrete water channel, either follow the by-wash going with the flow onto Derwent Dam or descend to the road, reaching the toilets and information centre at Fairholmes [172893]. Cycles can be hired here, weekend buses run up the valley to The King's Tree at the Howden Reservoir or, on Summer Sundays and Bank Holiday Mondays, buses run to Manchester, Glossop, Sheffield and Castleton.

11

Dambusters March

Eight-mile circuit in the Derwent Valley, starting from Fairholmes beside Ladybower Reservoir.

On Summer Sundays and Bank Holiday Mondays, Fairholmes is served by buses from Manchester, Glossop, Sheffield and Castleton. Alternatively, walk from Edale Station. Daily buses to and from Castleton, Bamford Station and Sheffield turn the A57/A6013 corner, close to the line of the walk.

Dark Peak map required.

Walking on tracks and paths with several steep ascents. The Derwent Edges are exposed to extremes of weather. In low cloud route finding is difficult.

From Fairholmes take the track, forking off the valley road. This crosses the bridge at the head of Ladybower Reservoir [172895]. Leave the road, and walk north across open grassland to the foot of Derwent Dam where water may be cascading over the high masonry wall. At the foot of the dam, turn east and ascend steps to the head of the dam. A path above water level runs to join a dirt road. This road is followed up the valley, crossing Hollin Clough. Gores Farm is visible across the water.

The next culvert drains Walker Clough [173909]. Peak and Northern Sign 191 points the way to Strines and Bradfield. Take this path. Stockport CHA added a dedication to George Watson and Geoffrey Price in May 1993. Ascending from the clough through Shireowlers

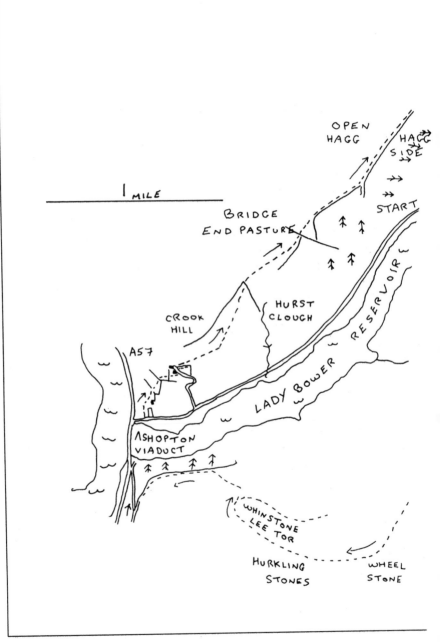

OPEN
HAGG

HAGG
SIDE

START

I MILE

BRIDGE
END PASTURE

HURST
CLOUGH

CROOK
HILL

A57

LADY BOWER RESERVOIR

ASHOPTON
VIADUCT

WHINSTONE
LEE TOR

HURKLING
STONES

WHEEL
STONE

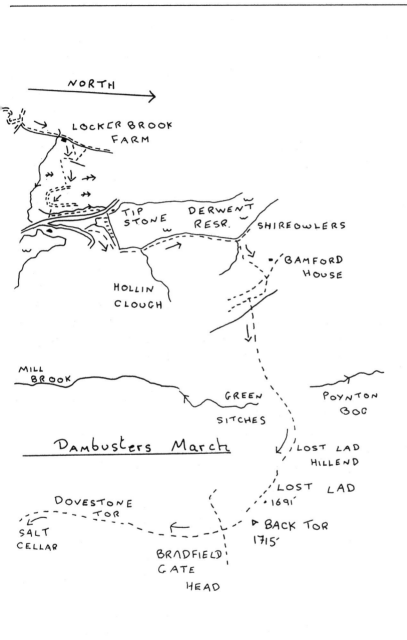

Plantation, the steep path switches back up the hillside. On the skyline a finger post comes into sight. When the walk turns to face north, a ruined cabin, Bamford House, can be seen. Reaching the skyline, a track from Abbey Bank to Mill Brook is crossed. Walking east following the direction finger to Derwent Edge, the path rises onto the ridge between Abbey Brook watershed and the Derwent.

Going towards a fence, the path crosses grass land before heading south to a ladder stile and gate [181911]. Over the stile the track crosses grass moorlands going east to the ridge between Cogman Clough and Green Sitches. The ground is dry, despite the proximity of Poynton Bog. This track reaches the Yorkshire-Derbyshire boundary, visible on the ground as a ditch. The right of way to Bradfield has turned away south east and the path to Lost Lad follows the ditch to Lost Lad Hillend [191914]. The summit is surfaced with flagstones which were airlifted in to check erosion. A stone causeway crosses wet ground to the summit of Lost Lad. Here, legend has it, a shepherd's son was lost one winter and, before dying of exposure, he scrawled the words "lost lad" on an exposed rock. In later years a cairn was erected, now there is a view-finder in memory of Baxby, ex. Sheffield Clarion Rambler [193912].

To the south east the white trig pillar of Back Tor is visible. The restored path runs to the boulders at 1765 feet and the pillar OSBM. S2145. Weather permitting, this is an exceptional view point. Look down the Derwent Edges; across Bleaklow, Kinder is visible, as may be Black Hill beyond Longdendale. Turning east, there is no comparable high ground for hundreds of miles, across the North Sea and beyond Denmark and Poland, as far as The Urals!

From the summit boulders a restored path heads south down the Derwent Edge. The right of way is crossed at Bradfield Gate Head, then to the left are the weathered cluster of rocks, Cakes of Bread. Following the flagstone path, the walker is indebted to the National Trust for surfacing a route which in wet weather often involved wading through peat pools. After Dovestones Tor, the restoration ends, but the path survives on top of the gritstone edge, the track worn down to sand and rock. The next group of stones, close to a ruined wall, is home to the large eroded rock pillar, Salt Cellar [196892].

Beyond the boulders at White Tor, the path begins to curve around the head of Grainfoot Clough with views down to the reservoir and Wheel Stones to the left. The path slowly descends and makes towards the west, past Hurkling Stones to Whinstone Lee Tor. From here there are views east to the A57 at Moscar and south to the square cut cliff of Bamford Edge.

At Whinstone Lee Tor a bridle road rises up onto the moor. At this point begin to descend. A steep path drops down a stony gully [198874], turns south, keeps descending to the wall and follows the wall across the top of the forest. There are views through the trees to Ashopton Viaduct. The path runs into the woods, goes east to join a logging track then goes through a gate onto a better surfaced road where a turn to the west leads past Ding Bank Farm [198865] onto the A57.

Cross the viaduct and go right into the valley road. Opposite the bus stop is a kissing gate. Enter the fieldand walk up to the springs [191865]. From here climb to Crook Hill Farm. The path bears north west, passing close to barns, possibly Toadhole Cote. Go through one gate way to a higher wall where, after the ladder stile, a National Trust sign requests a detour around the farm. Obligingly go through the right-hand gate and continue climbing to the corner of a barn. Behind here the path reaches the farm drive, cross, go through another gate and head to the distant uphill corner where the bridle road to Open Hagg is rejoined [186870].

The bridle path heads north, giving views across to Wheel Stones, then it rises onto the back of the ridge making for the restored wall north of the twin rocky peaks forming the summit of Crook Hill. Go through a gate and rise to the smooth grassy summit of Bridge End Pasture at 1280 feet [178878]. Over the rise, views now show the end of Ladybower Reservoir in the Ashop Valley.

One more gate then off the pastures, and the track runs to the forest fence, which is followed to a junction of ways before climbing over Open Hagg to a major cross roads above Hagg Farm [164890].

Turn north to Lockerbrook Farm where the forest thins. Enjoy views across to the Derwent Edge and down onto the reservoir. Pass the farm, and in fifty yards go over a stile in the fence. The path from here crosses grass land to the forest. Enter the woods, go down to the wall, bear right and locate the steep path descending to the logging road. Turn down the road and locate a footpath sign around the bend. Continue down to the watercourse [1708G6292]. Go with the flow and follow this channel to Derwent Dam.

Reach the road, go to the dam, look through the gate and note two plaques. One, unveiled on 16th May 1988, commemorates the night of 16-17 May 1943 when Lancasters of 617 Squadron took part in the Dambusters Raid. Guy Gibson's men had practised here at Derwent. The lower memorial, erected by public subscription, makes mention of Barnes Wallace and his bouncing bomb. Go up the road for a hundred yards to a second poignant memorial. It is in memory of the dog Tip who stayed with the body of his master, Joseph Tagg, on the Howden Moors for fifteen weeks from December 12th 1953 to 27th March 1954.

Return to the dam. After the gates, by a lay-by on the left, a path leaves the road and descends into the valley from where the return to Fairholmes is made.

12

Noe Return

Four-mile circuit from Bamford

Bamford lies on the railway linking Manchester to Sheffield. It has daily buses from Sheffield to Castleton, and on Summer Sundays and Bank Holiday Mondays buses from Manchester and Glossop pass the station.

Dark Peak map and Landranger Sheet 110 required.

Paths and lanes with two gentle ascents.

From Bamford Station, go onto the A6013 and turn north towards the village. Saltersgate Lane is passed, and in a quarter of a mile a track signposted to the Quaker Retreat goes west and crosses the Derwent. Go over the river and along the lane to The Retreat, a large stone building. Letters carved at roof level say that this once was the headquarters of the Derwent Valley Water Board [202830].

Passing the building, and before the car park a path on the right turns north to Thornhill. It crosses the route of the standard gauge railway constructed through the Derwent Valley during the building of the reservoirs. Take the path as it slowly ascends through the woods, in part following a sunken lane, and finally emerge onto the corner of Thornhill Lane and Carr Lane by the phone box [199834]. Pass Nicholas Hall on the left, noting the V.R. post box. A former church, complete with burial yard, stands on the corner of Slack Lane. Thornhill Methodist Church, a little distance down Slack

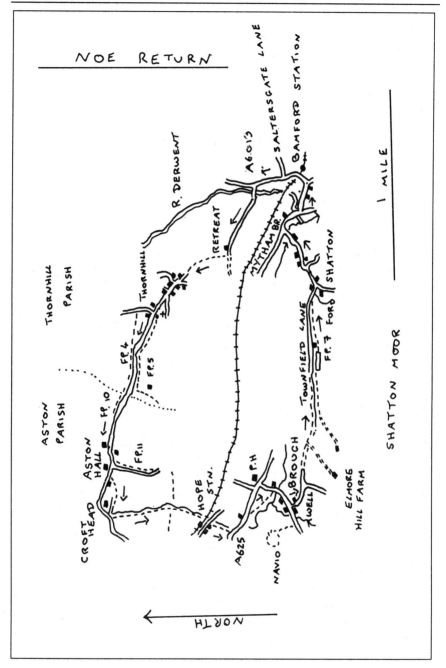

Lane, was of the Primitive Methodist faction, and dates from 1849. Opposite the chapel there is a mounting block dated 1834.

Follow the road up to Townhead Lane and Ryecroft Farm [197836]. Notice the stile opposite Townhead Lane. Here path Thornhill 5 follows the tarmac road, but over the hedge, where fences or hedges run up from the south to meet the lane, stiles are provided which allow the path, to be followed. This is as an option to walking the lane

Continue towards Aston. After a belt of timber on the right, path Thornhill 4 comes to meet the road. This also runs parallel with the lane. Thus, for the last two hundred yards to the parish boundary, the lane has a right of way on either side, but remote from it. The path on the northern side has several old stone stiles on its length. To the south of the road stands a ruin at Ryecroft, and a few yards past here the southern flanking path heads south out of Thornhill Parish. When this departure has occurred, the road enters Aston Parish [191838]. The right of way to the north of the lane continues as Aston 10, finally coming onto the lane through another old stone stile.

The lane descends through a rock cutting, and in a yard on the right spring water drips through rocks into a trough opposite Well Croft. The road rises to the junction at Aston Hall. Note that opposite here, where Aston Lane turns south, there is a stile, another path, Aston 11 turns south, again shadowing a lane for several hundred yards.

Pass the hall and go down into the stream valley. After the culvert [184840], climb steps on the left into the field and walk west. Pass Croft Head, dated 1886, and go onto the drive of Kilncroft which leads to the road. Reach the drive end [182839], go over a stile on the left and follow the stream south. Just inside Hope Parish, path 12 follows the stream down through three fields towards the railway. Don't cut across to the platform, go into the corner of the lowest field where the stream culverts below the line and cross the footbridge [182832].

From the bridge go onto the lane, now a BOAT, bridle way open to all traffic (see the 'Parishes, Paths and Partnerships' section, later in this book. Go east, passing the houses, then down off the lane to the culvert mouth. Follow the stream, avoiding the low willow limb, and eventually reach Station Road, A625. On the main road go east, passing The Paddock. When the road turns the bend, cross, and from the sign and stile walk the field path to the Noe. Cross the field to Bridge End Farm [184826].

From the footbridge see a date of 1824 on the central buttress then look upstream. The Noe is held back by a weir, the water wheel visible against the floodlit mill wall. Cross into Brough up the B6049, and after Mill Cottage turn left into Brough Lane.

Discover St. Ann's Well, 1859 [183825]. The source spring is in a gated fold behind the trough. From the adjacent St. Ann's Cottage, take Brough Lane east, rising, then forward along the rougher track. Go through two gates, steeply rising to a vantage point with views across to Thornhill, Aston, Win and Lose Hills. The track levels below Elmore Hill Farm and is joined by the drive of Shatton Hill Farm. The rolling bulk of Shatton Hill and Shatton Moor are resplendent to the south and east.

The track, Townfield Lane, is in a deep cutting, one vehicle wide. A rough road has recently been constructed on its southern flank. This is path Brough and Shatton 7. When the two roads converge, the right of way still runs parallel with the lane. Follow it between the fence and the plantation. At the coppice end, skirt to the south of the barn then walk parallel with the lane until a kissing gate is met. Descend steps, and go with the lane down through the shale cutting into Shatton [199823].

Cross the ford, turn left and pass through the hamlet. Go left at the next junction to cross the Noe at Mytham Bridge, and onto the A625 and east passing the garden centre to the Derwent. Downstream of this bridge, the Noe and Derwent merge. Immediately over the Derwent, go left on a traffic-free road back to the bus turning circle adjacent to Bamford Station. Here [208825] stand three massive stone shafts with an explanation board. These toll gates used to stand close to Mytham Bridge on the turnpike through the Hope Valley. The walk ends where it began, with various transport options.

13

Hope Hop

Four-mile circuit from Hope Station

Hope Station is on the railway from Sheffield to Manchester via New Mills. Nearby, on the A625, regular buses link Castleton to Sheffield. Less frequent are buses to Tideswell. Summer Sundays and Bank Holiday Mondays bring buses from Manchester and Glossop into the Hope Valley.

Dark Peak map required.

Paths and lanes. The route is sometimes churned by horses and sheep. No gradients.

From Hope Station car park, take the minor road running east into Aston parish. After the right-hand houses, a path starts at the stream culvert mouth [182831] and follows the parish boundary down onto the A625. On joining the road, go east, passing The Paddock. After the bend, cross and locate a sign and stile. Go into the field where the faint path runs south east past a meander on the Noe to Bridge End Farm, joining the B6049 at the bridge [183826].

Cross the river, noting the date of 1824 on the central buttress. Look upstream to where the river is held back by a weir, a floodlit water wheel hugs the side of the mill. Pass the mill into Brough. After Mill Cottage, Bradwell Brook is crossed at Burghwash Bridge. Look right for a V.R. post box and Peak and Northern sign. Signpost 38, dating from 1909, stands at an altitude of 616 feet. The sign marks the start of a path to Hope via Anavio. A lower sign makes mention

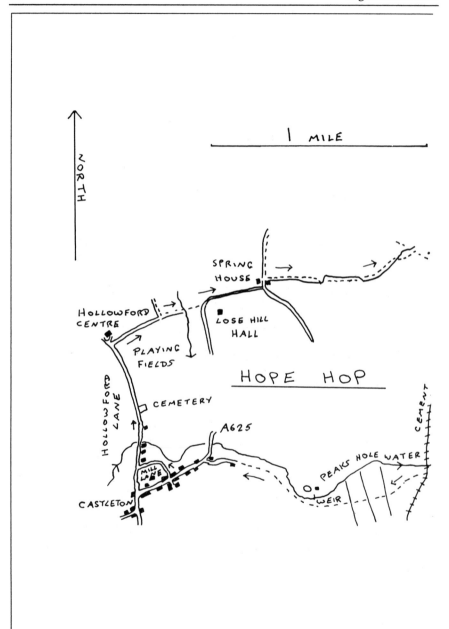

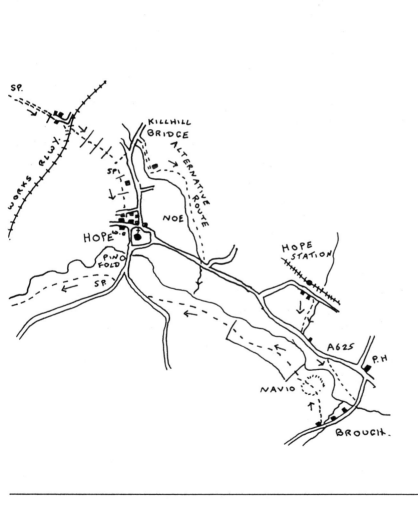

of the path to Hope Station, the route we have taken to reach this point.

Go into the field, rise to the ladder stile and cross the site of a Roman garrison [181827]. It was built at the confluence of two Roman Roads we have met on other walks. One is Batham Gate, literally the road to the bath, where bath indicates the hot water springs of Buxton or, to the Romans, Aquae Arnemetiae.

Arnemetiae was possibly the Latinization of a Celtic name for the goddess of the spring. The conjecture is that when the statue of the goddess was found, the inscription was illegible except for the first three letters which were read as Ann, by mistake. Hence the Buxton well's current name. The other road to Anavio came via the Hope Woodlands from Melandra. Relics from the fort are stored at Buxton museum. Unlike Melandra, the site has scant remains; no foundations from towers, walls or internal buildings.

The path cuts across the site, rising slowly and following a belt of woodland planted to screen the quarry workings to the south. Generally, it is a wide path which rises through gateways until at the top of the rise, the path drops into a wooded gully. Go through a gate onto open hillsides with views across Hope. After a downhill length it becomes gravel-surfaced and runs out onto Eccles Lane [172832].

Go downhill to the junction with Pindale Road, up the latter and discover a Peak and Northern sign on the right. From here the path to Castleton is surfaced through the first field where it contours above the wooded banks of Peaks Hole Water. Well-stiled and well-trodden, the path runs to the standard gauge cement railway linking Earl's Sidings on the main line to the cement works, whose chimney dominates the Hope Valley scene. Beyond the railway, the path crosses several walls until it runs beside the stream. Having crossed the parish divide into Castleton, pass the weir on the brook where water can be run off into the circular lagoon and pumped into the Ladybower supply system.

Follow the path as it becomes a lane and reaches Castleton Road [154831], A625. Notice a Peak and Northern sign dated 1908, complete with altitude. Twenty four feet have been lost since the walk left Brough. Go towards Castleton, staying with the road which leads to the bus station and toilets.

Before the bus station, on the right, stands the Swiss House Hotel. A right turn immediately past here leads into Mill Lane. Use this to avoid the village, and skirt around into Hollowford Road. Hollowford Road is followed to Trickett Gate House. Cross Peaks Hole Water and the road slowly rises, passing the Cemetery. Hollowford Training and Conference Centre [148835] stands at a fork in the road.

At the junction, turn north east along the track behind the rugby field. This gives views across the valley to Peveril Castle, Cave Dale and the cement works. The track runs level, and eventually turns north. At this point, following the signpost's direction, keep heading east along the field hedge until a stream is crossed and the road behind the National Park Study Centre, Lose Hill Hall, is met [152838]. The farmland to the north slowly rises to Lose Hill.

Passing behind Lose Hill Hall leads to castellated Spring House at the head of Warehouse Lane. After Spring House, turn uphill, then, after the stable block on the right, take a path east. This follows the hedge and fence. Go through a stile, keeping the uphill hedge to the left. After another stile the path moves onto more level ground between trees, skirting a trough. There is a further stile then at the top edge of more sloping land, a path descending from Lose Hill is met [164842]. This path is followed to a depression, possibly an old sunken lane. At intervals the path enters the sunken way, then leaves when the old track is totally infilled. Coming to the next farmstead, note an additional plate to the footpath sign in memory of Frederick H Fox of Sheffield Clarion Rambling Club, 1912-1962.

Walk through the farm and onto the lane. Go through the stile which leads to a footbridge over the cement railway. Over the mineral line, the walk finishes by running through a number of old strip fields, so there are plenty of stiles to surmount. This walk has two possible endings.

Close to Hope there is a Lose Hill sign [171838]. Either go east onto Edale Road, cross and descend to the Noe at Killhill Bridge.

Following the track downstream leads to the old mill and house where a river bank path runs to the A635 and Hope Station.

To finish in Hope, continue with the path into the estate, go forward and left at Shirley Close, through a paddock and into the village at a Peak and Northern sign dating from 1932 [172835]. It's interesting that on the post, secretary Thomas Boulger gave his address Brown Street, Manchester. {Boulger is commemorated at a footbridge over Hollingworth Brook between Chunal and Hayfield}

To reach the station it's a fifteen minute walk east along the A625, passing the cenotaph and the Noe at Netherhall Bridge.

Why Hope Hop? Whether it's Hope, Glossop, Ashop, Hassop or Alsop the "op" suffix is Anglo-Saxon, indicative of a small enclosed valley, or the upper part of a dale!

14

The Brindley Beat

Five miles around Wormhill Parish

Peak Dale is connected to Buxton and Stockport by hourly buses every day. The walk's starting point at Peak Dale is the Great Rocks Social Club on the corner of School Road and Batham Gate Roman Road, linking the A6 to the railway at former Peak Forest Station.

White Peak map required.

Field paths and quiet lanes with one ascent.

From the social club, turn the corner [087766] and follow School Road towards Upper End. The road passes Holy Trinity Church, the school and Meadow Avenue. It descends and forks at the phone box beside the war memorial. From here, at 1054 feet above sea level, go behind the memorial garden to a stile in the corner where a path runs into the field and turns west, rising up the pasture to reach Long Ridge Lane. On joining this ridge top road, formerly a major route from Derby to Manchester, go south east and two types of quarry will become visible. To the east are the extensive Tunstead Quarries with their faces and spoil heaps of white limestone. Closer to hand are the Waterswallow Quarries with dark stone on the spoil tips. The Tunstead Quarries extract limestone, hence this region's name of White Peak. The Waterswallow Quarry extracts basalt, a volcanic rock injected into the limestones in the geologically recent past. The volcanic intrusion gave the land its minerals, especially lead, and the heat from the extant eruptions still warms many thermal springs.

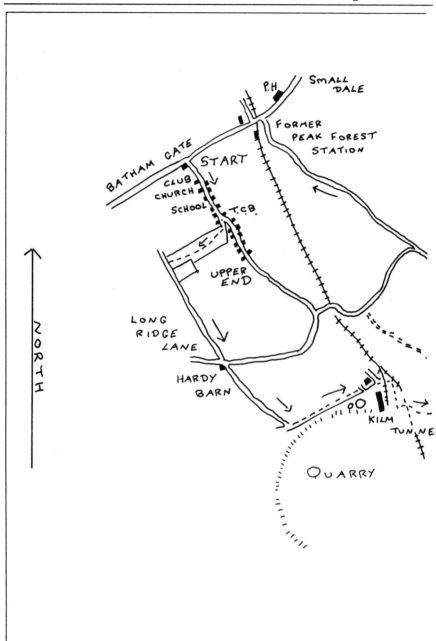

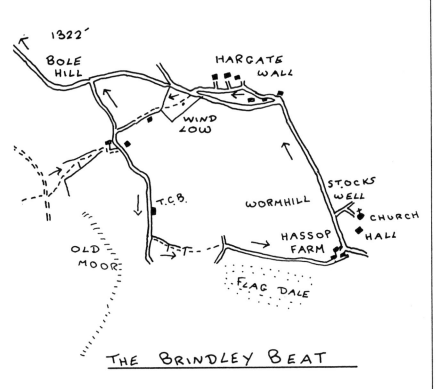

THE BRINDLEY BEAT

At Hardy Barn [089752] cross the road and continue along a green lane to the signposted path junction on the quarry rim. Turn west and descend onto the quarry floor. Signs warn of blasting times and concrete igloos are there for shelter if caught out by the blasting. The 1966 Guinness Book of Records identified this quarry as the largest in the United Kingdom. Over the past twenty nine years, as the quarry lies outside the National Park, it has continued to grow, possibly it still ranks as a superlative. The well- marked path drops into the valley close to settling lagoons [098748]. Pause here to watch the activities on the quarry floor: ready mixed concrete handling, pre-cast concrete fabrication, burning and crushing. Away to the west, the Old Moor is still being consumed by the demand for limestone. Cross the first road, go over the second beside the Tunstead Kilns and then over a gantry bridge. The waggons emerging from the massive kiln complex get an automatic wash, over the railway where trains shunt up and down finally exit from the quarry into dusty green fields.

The path goes down the track side before rising to cross a tunnel mouth through which Manchester to London via Derby trains once used to speed. It now carries the mineral trains into and out from Buxton. Using steps equipped with a hand rail, the path climbs over the tunnel and ascends a rocky hillside to meet a wide track [104747]. Here climb the stone and timber stile over the wall. The path scrambles up through rocks onto the hill top and follows close to the power line, making north east to Taylor Farm, Tunstead. Through gaps in walls some ten yards north of the power line, the walk goes to the barns where a corner signpost [108749] directs the path around the south of the farm to the road. Turn uphill and discover a plaque in the field. Erected in November 1958 by Derbyshire Archaeology Society, the stone celebrates the life of James Brindley 1716-1772. The famous canal engineer was born in a cottage at Tunstead, but it no longer exists. Turn south down the road, beware of the dog!

Reach Central Cottages and a phone box described as Tunstead Village, Wormhill. There is visible activity on the quarry top, an indication of how much land will be removed in the next few years.

Continue past the houses and look left for a stile. Here a path turns east [111744] and follows the wall towards Flag Dale. Cross various walls and as the dale develops head for a finger post visible on the valley's northern rim. This gives access to a lane which runs east to yards at Hassop Farm. From the first yards go through a gate on the left and exit, near the green, corrugated shed, onto the lane. At the Wormhill sign, turn uphill into the village. Looking right, see Wormhill Hall, and the helmet steeple of St. Margaret's Church.

The first building on the left, Well Head, stands opposite the village well. On the well is a plaque dated 1875, in memory of James Brindley, civil engineer, born in this parish 1716 AD. Wormhill's well dressing is the last week in August. On the other side of the well a limestone block bears a further Brindley plaque, positioned here in 1989 by the Institute of Civil Engineers, assisted by I.C.I. Chemicals and Polymers.

Follow the road north through the village, on the right stood the Bagshaw Arms and further on lay the school house. Walk uphill to the lane junction [121750]. Cross the road and bear west through Hargatewall. Pass Hillgreen Farm and Hayward Farm. This is a secluded, little known locality. The lane reaches a minor road, cross over and go through a stile. Beside the path stands the tumulus of Wind Low [115752] with a socket stone on its crest, which once held a cross or possibly a dipping stone from the plague days. From Wind Low the path aims west over a stile in the field corner. Walk down past a barn into the lane, skirting north of the farm and onto the road. Turn north to the junction with a busier lane [108754] and west, rising to 1238 feet on the tip of Bole Hill.

Keep with the road as it turns to the north. Views stretch across to Upper End and down to the Tunstead Kilns. The lane descends to a junction, head north west, rising up the quieter of the two tracks before dropping to Small Knowle End [093768]. Here the railway at the former Peak Forest Station is crossed. Buses can be caught on the corner. Peak Dale Institute lies a quarter of a mile up the hill. Mondays to Saturdays, service 189 takes you through Upper End and Waterswallow Quarries to Fairfield en route to Buxton.

15

Grin Low and Ladmanlow

Four-mile circuit south of Buxton

Buxton station is served every day by hourly trains from Manchester
via Stockport. Many trains originate from Blackpool and pass through
Preston and Bolton before reaching Manchester. Express and local
bus services halt opposite the station or terminate at the market
ground.

White Peak map required.

Paths and lanes with two easy ascents.

From the station cross Spring Gardens bypass and follow the road
around onto The Quadrant. Descend to the traffic lights at the foot
of Terrace Road, and go along the foot of The Slopes, passing
Memorial, Crescent and St. Ann's Well. On reaching the corner of
Hall Bank and The Square, cross and follow Broad Walk between
hotels, rest homes and the park through to the Temple Road –
Macclesfield Road junction [055729].

Turn up Temple Road, looking for the community school on the
left. Pass the sports complex and enter a passage, College Walk,
which leads past the older college onto Green Lane. Cross Green
Lane, head east for fifty yards then walk up a drive and through a
farm, comprising two white rendered buildings, into the car park at
Poole's Cavern.

The cavern is Buxton's show cave, home to early man, frequented
by Romans and possibly visited by Mary Queen of Scots. The cave's

passages are all at one level, a feeder of the Wye flows through the interior. From the steps at the far side of the car park, climb up into Grin Plantation. A wide stony track rises up through the trees and the walk follows this track out of the wood onto sheep-cropped grass. The hummocks in the ground are caused by quarrying or mining. Ahead stands the round stone tower of Solomon's Temple, a folly named after Solomon Mycock who had it built on top of Grin Low in 1896.

The name "low", usually applied to high points in the Peak District, indicates a site where early man heaped up a burial mound. Such sites, when excavated, usually hold human remains, flint tools and pottery. Buxton Museum exhibits artifacts from a number of lows or tumuli. Climb to the top of the tower using the internal stone staircase. Look south west onto Axe Edge, then north to see Buxton cradled between the hills. From the tower go west along the ridge to a gate way. Here a well-used track, still heading west, makes its way down the limestone hillside to cattle sheds and exits onto Grin Low Road.

Walking west leads to a junction with the A53 at Ladmanlow, and buses return to Buxton from here. Turn into Leek Road at the sign "Leek 11, Stoke on Trent 22". There was once a railway line crossing at this point. The Cromford and High Peak Railway connected the Peak Forest Canal at Whaley Bridge with the distant Cromford Canal. The Act of Parliament for this railway, rope-hauled on the inclines, horse tramway on the level, was granted in May 1825. On July 7th 1831 the line opened between Whaley Bridge and Hurdlow via Ladmanlow. When the passenger and freight line connecting Buxton to Ashbourne was sanctioned in 1890 it was intended to link with the Cromford and High Peak Railway three miles from Buxton. When this junction was completed in 1892, the inclines and tramways through the Goyt Valley to Ladmanlow closed.

Ladmanlow goods station survived for a number of years because there were several works established beside the line at Harpur Hill. The route to Stanley Moor Reservoir was in use until 1967.

On the right is a metal kissing gate [041717]. Go into the field and turn uphill. Pass the wall of Terret Reservoir and go through a gate

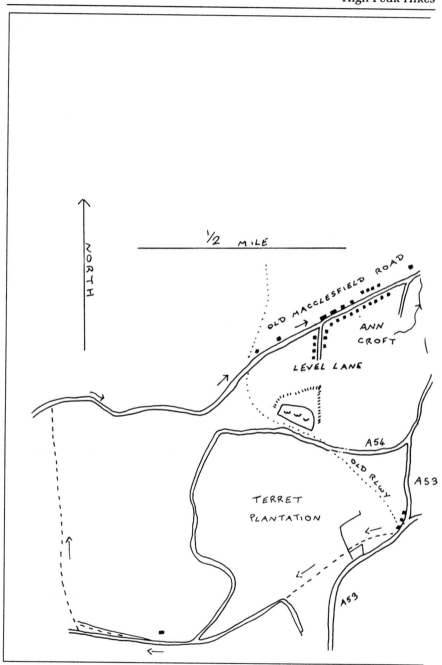

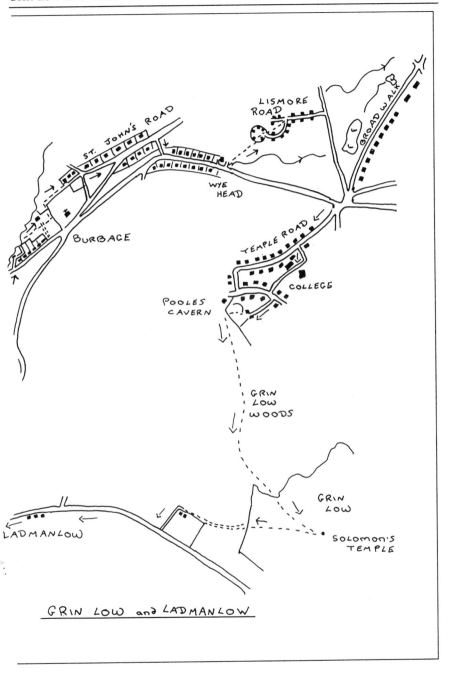

GRIN LOW and LADMANLOW

which is often tied. Out of Buxton into Hartington Upper Quarter, the path rises below Terret Plantation where stood the tumulus Ladman Low from which this area takes its name. Walk directly up the slope and onto a rough road connecting the A53 to the A54 [036715].

Half a mile away lies the summit of Axe Edge, 1810 feet above sea level, and the thirty fifth highest summit in the Pennines, ninth highest point in the Peak District. Private moorland within the National Park. One claim to fame for Axe Edge is the flashing of a heliograph from Snowdon to Axe Edge and onto Lincoln Cathedral. 110 miles line of sight each way!

The lane is followed west to join the A54 at a tower, possibly connected to the water table of the hill. The walk has come off limestone onto gritstone and the moor is underlain with coal seams. At 1500 feet above sea level, follow the main road for a hundred yards then follow the wall on the road's northern edge until a path heads north [028713]. Cross the moor, passing several coal mining depressions and the site of a former engine house, until the old Macclesfield Road is met.

Turn down the track, the A54 turns to run close, but stays on the southern side of the valley. Note that the valley is spanned by an embankment carrying the former Cromford and High Peak Railway. Look at the bridge portal where the railway passed below the old road. Burbage Reservoir is constructed adjacent to this embankment.

The road passes Level Lane, named from a mining level where water supplies have been obtained. The Wye is formed by the streams draining off the moorland. After descending past Anncroft Road, the infant river is crossed at Dog Hole Bridge, the water ochrous, possibly stained by the coal workings.

One footpath, Buxton 36, requires walking to preserve it. Discover this path by turning left after Dog Hole Bridge, and going down the drive of Brookside Cottage [041727]. The drive runs to the cottage. Here look right for a narrow passage between the Macclesfield Road gardens and Brookside Cottage's garden. This passage runs between bushes, turns left to The Wye and follows it down stream and into rough grass.

Turn away from the stream and, passing south east of the caravans and blue Nissen hut, walk between conifers to reach a cottage drive. Cross this drive and walk across rough grassland to the cemetery wall. Turn down the wall side and over a stile [043729], following the cemetery wall north east until the path is sandwiched between garden fence and wall. In this narrow stricture it dog legs beside the bowling club and exits on the corner of Bishops Lane and Nursery Lane at a footpath sign.

Walk forward into St. John's Road, cross, and head towards Buxton. Beside house 91, locate the passage Broomsway which leads onto Macclesfield Road. Turn down Macclesfield Road to Wye Head. On the left a source of the Wye emerges into daylight, having first been seen in Poole's Cavern. A path from the spring runs to the new houses at Lismore Park [051731], where a passage beside no. 10 leads to Lismore Road and Burlington Road. Across the latter stands The Pavilion Gardens, walk through these back to the centre of Buxton.

16

Discover Dove Holes

A three-mile circuit around Dove Holes

Dove holes has a rail service from Manchester, Stockport and Buxton.
Frequent daily buses run to Stockport and Buxton with an express
service going further afield to Derby and Nottingham.

White Peak map required.

Footpaths and tracks, some neglected.

Dove Holes stands beside the A6 road at 1000 feet above sea level.
To the passer-by the land appears to comprise upland sheep pasture
and quarries, active or disused. At first glance there is nothing worth
seeing. First looks are often deceptive, as this three mile walk shows.

Starting from the railway station [074781], a street runs past
grocers' and newsagents' to form a junction with the A6 opposite
Dale Road. The Wheatsheaf and The Queens stand facing each other.
Cross the A6 and turn north, climbing slightly towards Hallsteads.
Go into the drive on the right leading to the Community Centre and
the headquarters of Buxton Mountain Rescue Team [077781]. Continue forward to the Rescue Team hut. Outside, on a replica trig.
pillar, a plaque says that the Princess of Wales opened the hut on
June 14th 1990.

At the play equipment, turn north across public open spaces,
either by track or across the mown grass, aiming to the rear of St.
Paul's Church. Skirt around the burial yard wall and come to the
Bull Ring [078782].

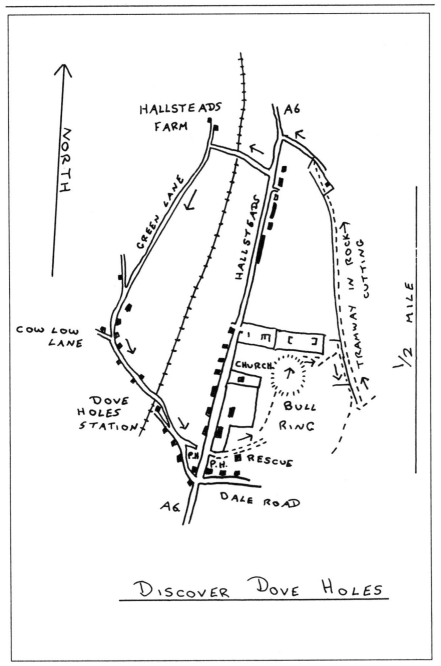

DISCOVER DOVE HOLES

Shown in Gothic script on the maps, indicative of an antiquity, the Bull Ring was a henge. In plan there is a central circular platform some fifty feet in diameter surrounded by a ditch, outside which is an earth bank. Dating back several thousand years, this structure would have had a ring of standing stones inside the ditch, used either as an astronomical calculator or for Druidical rites. Had the stones survived, Dove Holes would be as visited as Avebury in Wiltshire. Doubtless they were scavenged over the centuries for building

Continue north beyond the Bull Ring to reach a point between a cricket field and football pitch. Turn east and follow the line of the soccer pitch to the corner flag, the corner to the right as you face into the eastern goal mouth. From the corner, twelve paces lead to rough soil steps descending into a rock fissure. Take care as there is an unguarded cliff face. A rough path descends into the gully and makes to a stile. Go over the stile and down into a wide limestone valley. On reaching the wall running down the valley floor, go south, following the power line, over a stile by the bushes and through the gate on the left. Turn north, climb a stile and continue walking north up this narrow valley [080782].

We are following the upper section of the Peak Forest Tramway, constructed from the canal terminus at Bugsworth, passing through Chapel Milton and Barmoor Clough to reach the limestone at Dove Holes. The stone was taken away in horse drawn waggons, along the tramway and down the incline planes to Bugsworth where it was burnt in kilns prior to being shipped in barges to the mill towns of Cheshire and Lancashire. This transport system was functioning from 1799 to 1924. Ownership passed from the Peak Forest Canal Company to the Manchester, Sheffield and Lincolnshire Railway in August 1863, later becoming part of the Great Central Railway.

Heading north along the tramway we see the occasional sleeper, stones with bolt holes to which the shoe supporting the rail was fixed. The lines were constructed out of yard lengths of L section iron set apart at 4 feet 212 inches. This is the Outram Gauge, named after the canal and tramway engineer James Outram.

Continuing along the tramway the valley widens as the cutting walls are quarried away. The track narrows again. Look in the left-hand cliff for a crag of crinoidal limestone evincing that these hills were once thriving animal colonies below warm tropical seas, some two hundred and seventy million years ago.

On the right is a rough stile [080787], go over it and diagonally ascend the cutting wall, bashing through the nettle and grass to the side of a breeze block garage. Walk a few yards along the rim of the cutting, ahead a bridge carrying the A6 over the tramway is visible. The cutting top grass land is mown and used for putting. At a derelict railway waggon, go over the stile into a lane and follow the lane to the A6 [078789].`

Go onto the bridge for a last look down at the tramway. Notice an eroded township stone, possibly one side in the township of Bowden Head. Turn south onto Hallsteads and cross the road at the 30mph. sign. Take the lane on the right to the railway at bridge 74. By following the track you cross out of the limestone onto the gritstone. At the crossing of the Buxton line you have made the transition across the geological divide, go forward towards Hallsteads Farm and turn left [076788]. A green lane runs parallel with the railway. A few allotments stand below this lane. Eventually, emerge at a farm with an air-shaft into the freight line railway tunnel, turn left pass Cow Low Lane and descend back to Dove Holes railway station.

17

Dove Holes to Chapel en le Frith

Two miles beside Cow Low

Not every train stops at Dove Holes. Here is a scenic two mile walk to
Chapel en le Frith station over Cow Low, closely following the line of
Dove Holes Tunnel, now used by freight trains.

White Peak map.

Footpaths across farmland and rough-surfaced tracks.

From Dove Holes station [075781] go onto the road crossing the line,
and west, away from the village. At the junction, go up Cow Low
Lane, passing Highfield Avenue and the stone terrace of East View.
After the end house in Spring Bank Terrace, look for a stile on the
right [071784].

The path rises above the road, a spoil heap and air shaft are visible
to the north. Cross the stile in the wall and walk through the next
pasture, aiming for a gate. Pass below two power lines and locate a
stone stile in the wall fifteen yards north of the gateway.

Cow Low farm is visible. Aiming for the farm, go over a stone stile
in the next wall. The route heads to the front of the farm house
[068785]. Pass the garden wall and after skirting the first building,
turn right and through a gate into the yard.

Walk down the yard. After a building on the left, turn right off the
drive on a track heading north and slowly losing height. There are
two features to locate: away left stands a detached length of stone

wall on the flank of Cow Low, ahead an air shaft comes into view. At this point cross to the foot of the detached wall and contour around the flank of Cow Low on a faint path running at 1250 feet above sea level [065788].

Cow Low is a tumulus-topped summit. As the path is followed around the hill, views open out across Chapel en le Frith. The back drop stretches from Sponds Hill to Chinley Churn and Rushup Edge in the east.

In the valley below is a brick air shaft and the tunnel's northern portal, a hundred feet lower than the southern portal, one mile and 224 yards away in Dove Holes. The path skirts Cow Low to a stone stile. Climbing the wall, the skyline of Castle Naze is visible, as is the mast on Ladder Hill. Cross to a gate and stile, walk over a field to a wooden stile into a paddock and over another stile in the road side wall [061785].

Walk west along the road, passing trees in the top of Ridge Clough. Take a track on the right past Ridge Hall and Ridge Hall Farm [058788]. The lane runs through farmland into a final belt of wood-land, passes a Lodge and reaches the platforms of Chapel en le Frith station [055794].

There are hourly trains back to Manchester and Buxton.

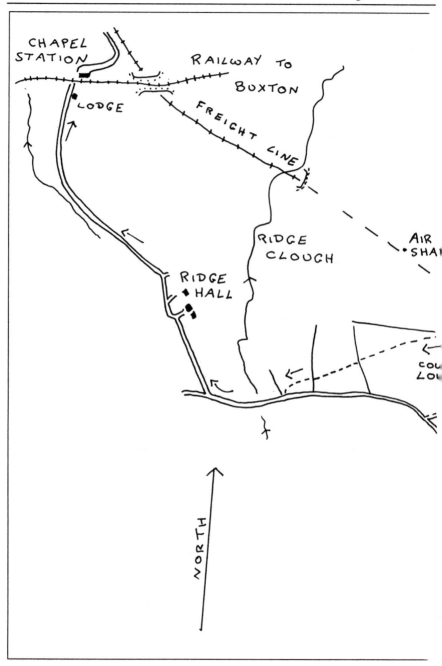

DOVE HOLES TO CHAPEL STATION

½ MILE

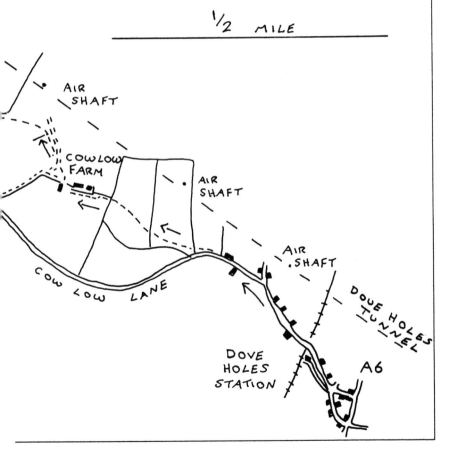

AIR SHAFT

COWLOW FARM

AIR SHAFT

AIR SHAFT

COW LOW LANE

DOVE HOLES TUNNEL

DOVE HOLES STATION

A6

18

Bagshaw and Bowden

A four-mile circuit around Chapel en le Frith.

The A6 bypass routes traffic around Chapel en le Frith. Buses linking Buxton to Stockport or Manchester to Nottingham pass through the town along the B5470.

Dark Peak map required.

Visible field paths, quiet lanes.

Between the bus stops at Town End and New Inn, lies Market Place with a Cenotaph and market cross [057807]. A little north east is the church of St. Thomas a Becket. The walk begins and ends here.

From outside the church gates, Church Brow descends to the road, and by turning left, the B5470 is followed towards Town End. Opposite the Council Office on the right is Hearse House, now converted into a Tourist Information Office. Continue past Moss View Garage and over a stream culvert. Here Warm Brook becomes the Smithy Brook, and a stone identifies the borders of Chapel and Bowden townships. Continue east to the Methodist Church at Town End [062808]. Turn right into the church yard and walk past the Sunday School which has been converted into houses, Wesley Court. Pass the burial yard into Warmbrook Road, and continue to Warmbrook School. The road bends right, take the road on the left, then go right into Thornell Close.

Pass the homes, ignore the flagged path on the left. Take the second left path, which is worn into the grassland. Go through the gate beside the stone house and up the field. The path is partly flagged. Aim towards a wall, and through the stile into an unsurfaced drive at Lower Eaves. Climb steeply to a tarmac road [065803].

Directly across the road take another path. The stile over the low wall is hidden in the grass and nettles to the left of the gateway. Fork left, passing stables and a cottage onto the drive at High Leigh. Glancing right, note the farm name, Top of the Plane. Walk across the drive, down towards iron gates then right in a narrow passage to a view point across the Blackbrook locality [068804].

Here the walk crosses an inclined plane on the Peak Forest Tramway, constructed circa 1799, enabling limestone from Dove Holes to descend to a horse tramway en route to the canal at Buxworth. Cross the inclined plane, descend stone steps into the field, and go over the stile in the lower wall. Follow the pasture wall to the right as it descends to the bypass. In the lower corner of the field a stile gives access to a grove of trees beside the bypass. Go right, south, until the pavement ends, then cross four lanes of traffic [070804]. On the opposite side, descend to a bridge spanning Barmoor Clough. Turn down stream past Blackbrook Farm and continue past Longdendale Nursery.

Look for Blackbrook House on the right. Immediately past the house's garden wall, identify a stile where stone steps climb the wall and step over a strand of plain wire. Once in the field, walk uphill, following the trees and wall to the pump house. A quality stile climbs into the enclosure, steps descend to the lane [071807]. The lane runs uphill, and below trees' roots cling to the rock walls. On the left is Laneside, enter the drive, climb steps in the wall on the right. Once in the field, turn left to the gate, go through and follow the wall to the right, walking up the Bagshaw valley [074809]. Over the stile in the next wall, pass a well with stone slab cover. At the broken wall, go down into the valley, aiming for the diagonally opposite corner. Here a stile gives access to the culvert.

Cross the valley floor, climb another stile then climb towards the barn gable at Bagshaw Hall Farm. By gate or stile join the track and turn east through the farm yard into Bagshaw [076811].

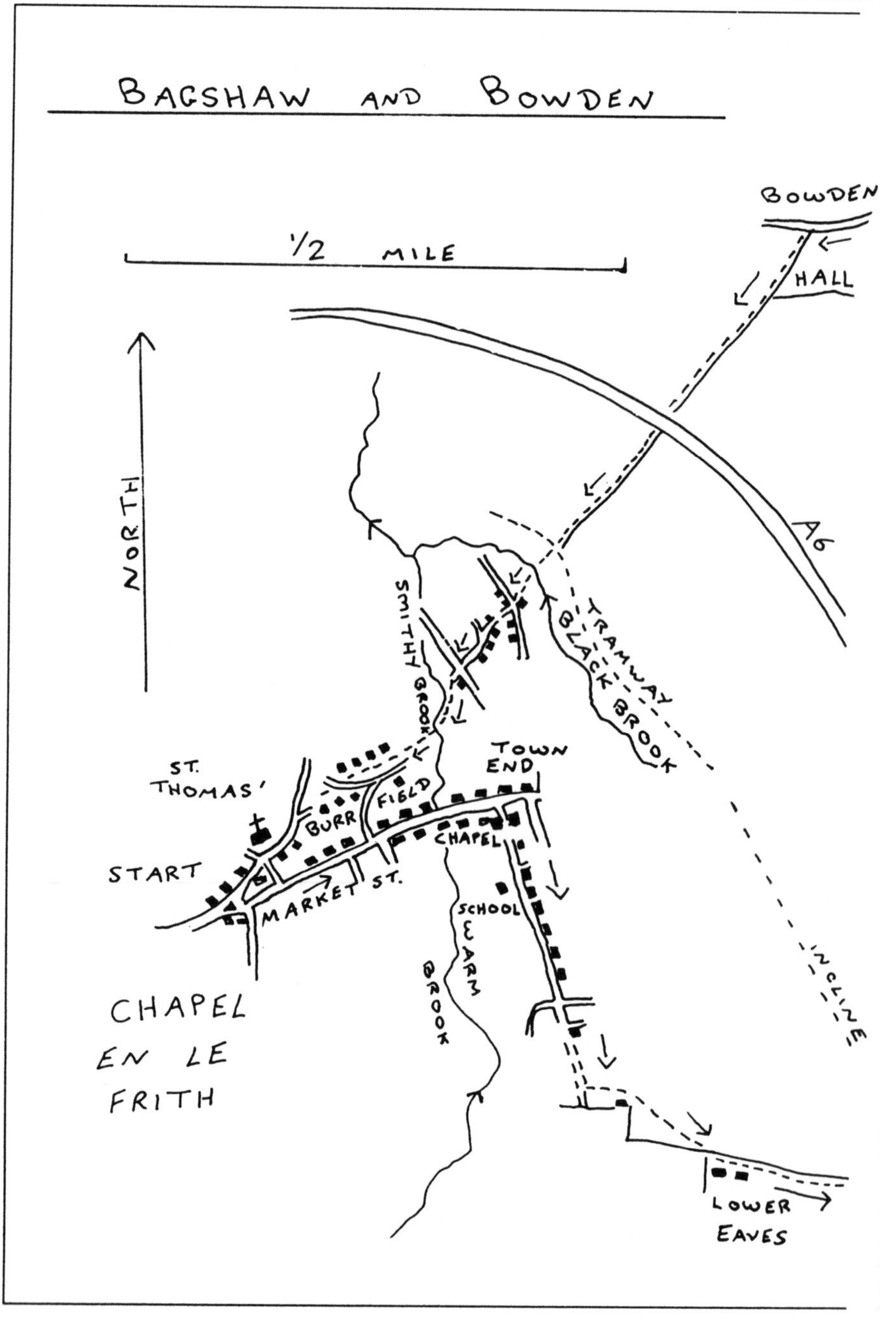

BAGSHAW AND BOWDEN

½ MILE

NORTH

BOWDEN

HALL

A6

TRAMWAY

BLACK BROOK

SMITHY BROOK

TOWN END

ST. THOMAS'

BURR FIELD

START

MARKET ST.

CHAPEL

SCHOOL FARM

CHAPEL EN LE FRITH

BROOK

INCLINE

LOWER EAVES

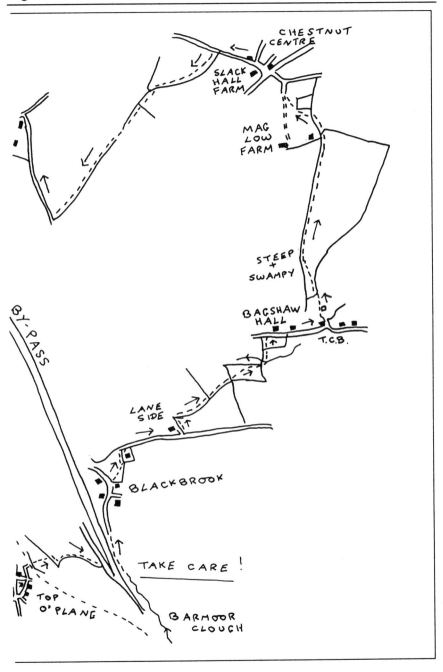

CHESTNUT CENTRE

SLACK HALL FARM

MAG LOW FARM

STEEP + SWAMPY

BAGSHAW HALL

T.C.B.

BY-PASS

LANE SIDE

BLACKBROOK

TAKE CARE !

TOP O' PLANE

BARMOOR CLOUGH

Continue through the hamlet. From the telephone box, continue uphill to the next houses. The end cottage is a Methodist Chapel, dated 1886 and still used by local residents. Return to the 'phone box and go right, past the house, to a gate. Walk up a track to farm ruins. Look up the slope for a finger post and stile giving access to a copse of trees. Once over the stile, cross a bridge spanning the swamp. The path climbs to cross another wet area on stepping stones then rises to drier land. Look for traces of a cobbled road then follow cattle tracks north to Maglow Farm. Keeping the farm on the left, pass the buildings into a gateway with exposed bed-rock [077817]. Go over a stile in the wall on the left and down onto the farm drive which is followed north to the cross roads at The Chestnut Centre. Detour through the gates at the Centre to see the Friend's Burial Yard, dating from 1668.

Back onto the lane, take the minor road climbing away from Slack Hall Farm. In a hundred yards, go through a gateway on the left [074820], and take a waymarked track into the field. Pass a few trees, go through the gate on the left, and walk the wall side to a further gate and descend to a copse. Go over the wall and follow it down towards the bypass. Reach a ladder stile and enter a narrow lane [069814]. Turning right leads to Bowden Hall. The hall, with cottage, barns and stables, offers eye-catching architecture. Turn down the road, looking for a gate on the left. From here the path runs to the bypass. Across the A6, the passage continues to a section of tramway linking the inclined plane to Buxworth. The path continues to cross Black Brook [062812] and reaches a lane. Cross, take a passage and pass a garden with ploughs, then a Bowden finger post and onto Hayfield Road. Across the road is a kissing gate. The final section of footpath crosses Smithy Brook and goes through Burrfields [060810], an open area becoming swamped by infill housing. The path runs onto the estate road. Cross and continue onto the church yard gates at the end of the walk.

19

Toddbrook and Taxal

Five miles around Whaley Bridge

Whaley Bridge has a regular rail service to Manchester, Stockport and
Buxton. Express buses run to Manchester, Buxton, Derby and Notting-
ham. Local buses run to Stockport, New Mills, Chinley, Chapel en le
Frith and Macclesfield.

Dark Peak and White Peak maps required.

Tracks and footpaths through fields, parkland and woodland.

From the railway, or the bus stops close to the Jodrell Arms [011815],
locate Reservoir Road. Commencing on the west of Market Street,
beside The Railway, pass below the railway bridge and ignore the
right turn into Whaley Lane. Walking ahead, following Reservoir
Road, the houses are left behind and the pavement follows a high
hedge. After the bend the road levels to pass Todd Brook Reservoir
[007812]. Cross the road and go over a footbridge spanning the
reservoir spillway. Walk onto the dam and cross the embankment
to the bridge over the central spillway. Cross the far side of the dam
to a stone stile. The dam was built in 1838-39 by the Peak Forest
Canal Company. It holds back the flow of Todd Brook and feeds
untreated water down to the canal at Whaley Bridge basin. Looking
upstream, the water stretches up into a wooded valley, the south
western skyline comprises Taxal Edge. Looking north east from the
centre of the dam, Chinley Churn is the obvious high ground, Mount

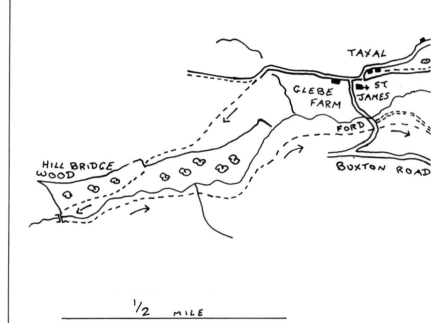

TAXAL

GLEBE
FARM

ST
JAMES

FORD

HILL BRIDGE
WOOD

BUXTON ROAD

½ MILE

TODDBROOK and TAXAL

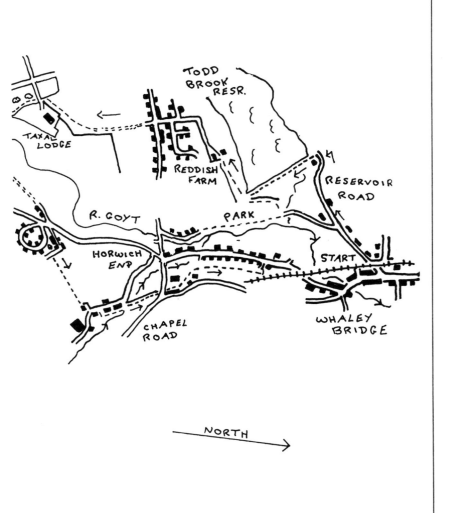

TODD BROOK RESR.

TAXAL LODGE

REDDISH FARM

RESERVOIR ROAD

R. COYT

PARK

HORWICH END

START

WHALEY BRIDGE

CHAPEL ROAD

NORTH

Famine and South Head can also be seen. Edale Rocks, on distant Kinder Scout, can be recognized.

Go over the stone stile onto a section of the Midshires Way running from Stockport to Aylesbury. The path follows the hawthorn hedge and passes over another stone stile into Reddish Farm yard.

From the yard, go along Reddish Lane, turn left and onto Maccclesfield Road [006806]. Crossing the road at the telephone box, the walk takes a track into the fields. Follow the track to a wet area where a spring fills a trough. The path turns up the field and reaches the hedge sheltering the grounds of Taxal Lodge School. Climb over a stile then turn left and cross the school drive. Walking below high trees, the path follows the fence to a rustic stile, and out of the woods into more open land. Fork right to crunch across the gravel forecourt of Chimes of Taxal, once a coaching inn [006799].

This brings you to St. James's, Taxal. The present structure, excluding the tower, dates from 1889. There have been Rectors of Taxal since 1287. Taxal was a daughter chapel to the mother church at Prestbury. The Church ceased to be dependent on Prestbury in 1377. Despite the boundary changes of 1936, when Taxal was moved out of Cheshire into Derbyshire, the Church still remains within the Diocese of Chester.

From the Church follow the lane past Glebe Farm, heading into the Goyt Valley. The route is surfaced and follows the Midshires Way. Descending slightly, the track comes to a gateway at Widow Clough. From here Whiteleas Road runs south to Overton Hall. In a few yards the road climbs to a finger post standing on the left [006794]. Leave the road and take a well-trodden path through the open pastures. It climbs slowly, rising to two stone gate posts. Deer are often grazing here.

From the stone posts take in the views across to Fernilee, west to the moorland and Taxal Edge, south back to Whaley and down the Goyt to the plateau of Cown Edge. The path forks. Keep left, aiming to the sign and stile at Hillbridge Wood.

Go over the stile to enter the Derbyshire Wildlife Trust Nature

Reserve. Keep with the path through the woods. Ford a streamlet, across exposed rock and pass through open woodland glades until the reserve is left, and a bridge on the left crossed, over the infant Goyt [011787].

Go over the river at Hill Bridge, then north, downstream, a path follows the valley floor and passes a Peak and Northern signpost. Climb over a fence and walk forward to a second stile. The woods are entered by the third stile and a path, restored in parts, runs through Shallcross Woods. At the end of the wood the path crosses a rough road [008799]. Below there is a ford and footbridge across the Goyt. This trail keeps level through the stile, across the track, and beside the last trees to a stile onto a wide track. This is followed through a gate out onto Buxton Road [010802].

Cross the A5002 into Mevril Road. Passing the houses, walk to the play equipment and look for a gap in the hedge. Take a path following a former pit tramway down hill to Wheel Farm on New Road. Half way down a bridge was built to enable cattle to commute from either field. At the lower end a steel derrick stump can be seen in front of the Scout Hut. Proceed onto New Road, turn left, and on the right find Cromford Court then a path through to Randal Carr Brook. A walkway runs between Cromford Court and the stream, and heron, dipper and kingfisher are often seen here. The track ends at a stone commemorating the Cromford and High Peak Railway [012805]. In the final stages of this walk keep to the old rail track as it runs below Chapel Road, through a tunnel, through the cutting then behind houses, ending close to the present railway line. A left turn brings you onto Buxton Road beside The Cock [011810]. Turning right and passing under the railway bridge leads into Market Street, Whaley Bridge. Pass the shops back to the The Jodrell. If time permits, go down Canal Street opposite The Railway and explore the canal basin.

20

Brand New

Ten miles by Dane, Dove and Wye

The Cat and Fiddle sits close to the Derbyshire — Cheshire border. Despite standing at 1690 feet above sea level, it is not England's highest inn.

A bus service running between Buxton and Macclesfield passes the Cat on Saturdays throughout the year. Extra services run on Summer Sundays. Utilising buses running between Buxton and Hanley along the A53, this walk can be split into two five mile sections. One can easily walk the two and a half miles from Buxton to The Cat by heading out to Burbage then along Macclesfield Old Road. This passes through Anncroft and skirts the head of the Goyt Valley until it joins the A537 close to the inn.

White Peak Map required.

Walking bridleways and lanes, plus a network of paths around Brand Side.

From the bus stop opposite the Cat and Fiddle [001719], a bridleway sign points the way. Follow a level, well-surfaced track across the moor. The track heads south and then swings around to face south east. After a mile, Peak and Northern sign 105 is met, offering an option of descending Cumberland Clough to Wildboarclough. Ignore this choice, stay with the track and enjoy views across the Stafffordshire Moorlands to the Roaches and over to Gun Hill. Possibly the only man made object in view, other than walls and fences, is the telecommunication tower on Croker Hill, visible over the ridge of Shutlingsloe.

The track descends, following a gully, through Danebower Hollow and reaches the A54 [010700]. Cross the road. At a finger post, descend, following the fence into the upper Dane Valley. Cross a track and descend to a solitary chimney. The map says it's an air shaft. I believe it to be a chimney, connected via a flue tunnel to a furnace lower down the hillside. All around are spoil heaps from the Reeve Edge and Danebower Quarries.

The track runs beside the Dane following the infant river down below Holt Farm. At a stile the path enters a field and threads through marshy valley bottom pasture until a wider track is joined and followed down the valley to Three Shire Heads [009685].

Here Cheshire, Staffordshire and Derbyshire come together. Old pack horse trails meet, and once would have forded the Dane at Panniers Pool. Now Pannierspool Bridge makes for an easier crossing of the river. Cross the Dane, and look under the bridge to see evidence of widening in the distant past. Pass across the Dane out of Cheshire into Derbyshire, and take the track following the clough running north west. The stream forms the county boundary. Banks of dark shales are visible. The track rises to a point below Blackclough. At a fork in the stream step out of Derbyshire into Staffordshire.

Providing access to Blackclough, a narrow tarmac lane is met, which is not visible on the White Peak Map [015689]. Follow this lane. To the north is the house at Gleadtail. The lane keeps close to the stream, which, tending east, continues to cut into the shales between Orchard Common and Knotbury Common. The lane rises. At the foot of a shale bank on the left, an ochrous spring, streaked with green weed, issues from a fissure [018687]. On large scale maps this is titled Alum Spring. Taste the water, it has an unpalatable metallic tang.

Above Alum Spring, the track climbs, crosses the brook and forks. Take the route to the right, heading south east over a ridge and down to Readyleech Green. The road from here heads south to another

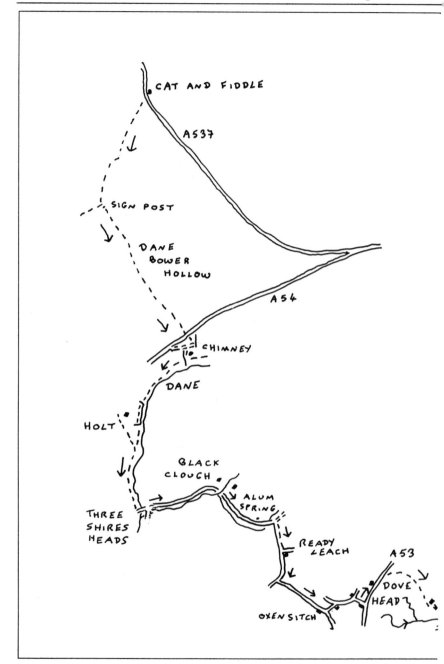

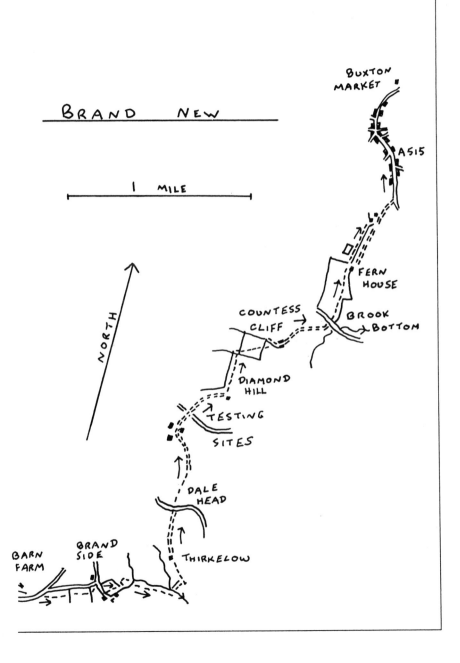

tributary of the Dane. Across the valley lies Wolf Edge, beyond which is Oliver Hill, the highest point in Staffordshire. Descend to the road junction, fork left, east, rise up past Oxensitch [027681] and turn north. A track climbs to Highfield, Hilltop and Hill End, reaching the A53 at Quarnford Lodge Guest House.

This accommodation, 4 miles from Buxton and 8 miles from Leek, is passed by four buses a day connecting Buxton and Hanley. Here, at the half way point on this walk, a return to Buxton could be made by bus, and the second half enjoyed another time.

Walk north along the A53, leave Staffordshire and enter Derbyshire. The cottage on the left, standing at 1520 feet above sea level, is called Dove Head [031684]. Below the road is the source of the Dove. I understand that somewhere there is a spring with a stone lintel initialled by Izaak Walton and Charles Cotton. Not an original. Walton, author of "The Compleat Angler" died in 1683.

After Dove Head the road rises. Go over a stile on the right into the rough pasture. A sweeping path descends down the hill, crossing channels of water which flow into the infant Dove. The path becomes a track, runs down to a gate and heads past Barn Farm [036684]. Continue down the farm drive to reach the river. Don't cross the Dove, go north east on a rough track. Go over a new stile on the right and take a path which follows the sunken lane rising up to Brand Top. The path passes through a stile. In the lane, a spring fills a bath. Continue uphill, and the path, still parallel with the lane, squeezes through a stone stile. From here enjoy the view of the Dove following a narrow valley down towards Washgate.

At the top of the fields the path squeezes through another stone stile into the lane. Continue to the Brand Top cenotaph within its enclosure [044685]. The names on the war memorial identify the farms from which the fallen were called, Allsopps is one I don't recognise. Beside the cenotaph stood a Methodist Chapel. Close to the telephone box is the school, dating from 1851 and now used for the parish meetings of Hartington Upper Quarter.

It is speculated that a Roman road from Buxton to Leek left Higher

Buxton, ran east of Grin Low and headed for Brand Top, before continuing on a straight line to join the A53 at Morridge Top.

From the cenotaph, walk the ridge top road south east to the buildings at Brand Top Farm. A path heads north east, don't confuse it with a route going through a wall stile with a daubed yellow arrow. Our path passes a circular pond and keeping north of Moss House, begins to drop into the valley. The land narrows and a sunken track heads down to a barrier of corrugated sheets. Stones to the right of this barrier enable it to be crossed. Go down the gully [046686], turn down stream, go over a stile and continue to the footbridge. No name is given to this brook but higher in the hills it drains out of Cistern's Clough.

Across the bridge, turn downstream. It may be drier to walk higher up the slope. A stile allows this feeder of the Dove to be followed. The stream lies close to the gritstone/limestone divide, and Hollins Hill is seen downstream. To the east are the limestone outcrops of Thirkelow Rocks. The stream cuts down into shales. At a lower stile go into marshy ground and follow the wall away from the river into the limestone. Climb [050687] to join a track, south of Thirkelow Farm. Joining the track, turn north and walk through Thirkelow. There are sweeping slabs of limestone to the right. Follow the drive to the High Edge road. A tumulus at 1416 feet above sea level is the Thirke Low, from which the rocks and farm are named.

On the lane [048693] turn left, take the second stile on the right. This leads into the Health and Safety Executive testing sites. The path heads into well-kept grass lands and is marked with green and white sticks. It leads to a turning circle on a tarmac track.

Follow the track and go over the stile beside the gate to a group of buildings. A sign directs the walker to the right, keeping with the main site road. At a crossing of the former Cromford and High Peak Tramway, [048702] take the road ahead signed to Countess Cliff. Follow the lane to hut 14, go left at a circular water tank and along the field edge to a gate at Diamond Hill [051708].

Walk off the test sites and cross the field on the right. A sign post at the next wall directs the path over two more walls into the yards at Countess Cliff Farm. Go through the yards, a final gate, and then the path, cutting corners off the rough drive, leads down to Brook Bottom. The stream to the east, polluted with material leached from old lime workings, is a feeder of the Wye, destined to make its way beside Duke's Drive into Ashwood Dale.

Having reached Grin Low Road, cross, proceed uphill for a few yards then go up into the field at the sign on the right [058712]. Cross a track and follow the wall north. After the stile head across the open pasture into a wide space between two beech woods. The ground falls towards Fern House. Follow the wall on the right, go through a gate and down a miry track to the stables.

At the gate nearest the farm locate a series of narrow stiles, one with a waymark that enables a muddy path be followed through a fence into an exercise paddock. Go out by a gate, ignoring the stile into the farm yard. Continue north, trying to keep the wall on the right. The path threads through a passage between paddock and wall, over another stile, then reaches Fern Lodge [059721]. At the octagonal wooden garden chalet, go over the wall to the cattle grid. Join Fern Road and follow it through open meadows to join London Road opposite the Haddon Hall Hotel.

Following London Road leads to the Dale Road traffic lights [058729]. Cross and go up High Street to Market Place, toilets and bus stops [058733].

Interlude

Parishes, Paths and Partnership

Derbyshire County Council have responsibility for the public rights of way within the County. The 1980 Highways Act states that the County Council, being the Highway Authority, has a duty to assert and protect the rights of the public to the use and enjoyment of any highway in their district, and to prevent, as far as possible, the stopping up or obstruction of those highways.

Under the term "highway" we can define a footpath as a highway over which the right of way is on foot only. A bridleway is a highway over which there is a right of way on foot or horseback, possibly with the additional right to drive animals. Parliament, in 1968, granted cyclists the right to use bridleways. A carriageway is a highway over which there is a right of way on foot, horse back, in or on a vehicle.

Other definitions in use are "RUPP" or road used as a public path. This makes obsolete the archaic categories "CRB" or carriage-road bridleway and "CRF" or carriage-road footpath. RUPPs are deemed not to have vehicular rights. If vehicular rights can be proven the route becomes a "BOAT" or byway open to all traffic.

The National Parks and Access to the Countryside Act, 1949, began the process of identifying the 140,000 miles of footpath and bridleway within England and Wales and defining laws vital to their protection. The County Councils were given the duty of surveying and mapping all public rights of way in their area, classifying them as bridleways, footpaths or roads used as public paths. Section 28 of the Act required the County to consult with District and Parish Councils. For Derbyshire a standard form was drafted and issued to the Parishes who completed one for each path surveyed.

From a study of the forms RW1 issued to Charlesworth it appears that the Parish Council purchased sheets of the six inch map covering the parish. The appointed surveyor then studied the map, looking where the cartographers had plotted paths, and went out to see if such paths were negotiable. The maps carry a disclaimer that the representation on the map of any road, track or path, is no evidence of the existence of a right of way (unless the map is overprinted with rights of way information). However, when the map was drawn a path must have been visible on the ground for the Ordnance Survey to map it out.

Having walked the paths, the parish surveyors filled in the form RW1, stating the Ordnance Survey sheet and edition used, gave a familiar name to the path if known, and gave a starting and finishing point for the path. Later in the form they provided a written description of the route, mentioning any gates, stiles and notices. Towards the end of the form the surveyor had to describe any restrictions to the use of the path, whether there was a right to plough over it or close it for a fair. Other questions evinced the years of uninterrupted public use, any repairs in the past and the general condition of the route. Finally, the names and addresses of the persons carrying out the survey were added and the date of the walk included.

Each path walked, where considered to be a public right of way, was given a draft number and its route marked on a draft map. When the parish survey was complete, these provisional details were made available for public comment. If no challenges were forthcoming the map and those paths identified were classed as Definitive. The Definitive Map and the unique Definitive Number for each path became conclusive evidence that, on the Relevant Date, there was a public right of way. The Relevant Date may vary from Parish to Parish. For example, Tintwistle is 1/2/55, Chisworth 1/6/54 and Glossop 1/6/54.

Having established the rights of way, the County Councils had to install an inspectorate to investigate claims of obstruction to rights of way. A legal apparatus was set up to deal with applications for closure, diversion or the redesignation of paths, plus the investigation of hitherto unsurveyed paths whose usage required them to achieve definitive status. There was also a need for a rolling programme of re-surveying Definitive Maps to keep them up to date, and for providing funds to maintain paths, provide new stiles, signs and bridges. A minor maintenance fund was allocated to those Parishes who wished to have an Agency Agreement. These funds, variable on the mileage of rights of way within the parish, were available for repair and restoration. One responsibility placed firmly on the County Council was the provision of a signpost at every point where a right of way joins a metalled road (Countryside Act 1968).

Thirty years after the Relevant Date for parishes within High Peak a cursory look around showed that many paths had never been sign posted at metalled roads; paths were obstructed; stiles and bridges had been missing for many years; parishes were not aware of their obligations or of available funds; and the Matlock- based footpath inspectorate struggled with a burgeoning workload.

This was not unique to Derbyshire. Throughout England and Wales the path network was in disrepair. To promote path awareness and restoration, the Countryside Commission focused the efforts of County and Metropolitan Boroughs into having all their rights of way furnished, signed and free of obstruction by the year 2000.

To kick start action within the County Shires, a Parish Paths Partnership was spawned. Here a designated officer would approach the Town and Parish Councils, encourage the councillors to survey their rights of way, evolve a project or scheme for path maintenance then obtain funding for these works, partly from County and Countryside Commission funds.

Inside High Peak, working under the Wildlife and Countryside Act of 1981 Section 53, the County Council began to re-survey the rights of way within the parishes. From the working copy correct at February 14th 1995, we can plot the number and mileage of rights of way within the constituent parishes:

Aston	13 Footpaths
	3.4 miles of rights of way.
Bamford	14 Footpaths
	3.8 miles of rights of way

Brough and Shatton	13 Footpaths 4.0 miles of rights of way
Buxton	81 Footpaths 1 Bridleway 2 RUPPs 26.5 miles of rights of way
Castleton	52 Footpaths 5 Bridleways 21.6 miles of rights of way
Chapel en le Frith	172 Footpaths 2 Bridleways 54.9 miles of rights of way
Charlesworth	104 Footpaths 2 Bridleways 42.6 miles of rights of way
Chinley, Buxworth and Brownside	79 Footpaths 1 Bridleway 25.8 miles of rights of way
Chisworth	30 Footpaths 1 Bridleway 10 miles of rights of way
Derwent	8 Footpaths 5 Bridleways 15 miles of rights of way
Edale	30 Footpaths 8 Bridleways 23.6 miles of rights of way
Glossop	169 Footpaths 4 Bridleways 30.6 miles of rights of way
Green Fairfield	9 Footpaths 1 Bridleway 5.9 miles of rights of way
Hartington Upper Quarter	137 Footpaths 6 Bridleways 1 RUPP 62.4 miles of rights of way
Hayfield	64 Footpaths 16 Bridleways 1 RUPP 43.4 miles of rights of way

Hope	38 Footpaths 5 Bridleways 19.7 miles of rights of way
Hope Woodlands	22 Footpaths 9 Bridleways 3.6 miles of rights of way.
King Sterndale	11 Footpaths 1 Bridleway 4.3 miles of rights of way
New Mills	156 Footpaths 18 Bridleways 13 RUPPs 52.7 miles of rights of way
Peak Forest	60 Footpaths 7 Bridleways 27.8 miles of rights of way
Thornhill	15 Footpaths 5 miles of rights of way
Tintwistle	18 Footpaths 1 Bridleway 7 RUPPs 18.9 miles of rights of way
Whaley Bridge	97 Footpaths 3 Bridleways 2 RUPPs 28.5 miles of rights of way
Wormhill	49 Footpaths 8 Bridleways 20.4 miles of rights of way.

In total, 1441 Footpaths, 104 Bridleways and 37 RUPPs giving a total of 584 miles of rights of way.

Currently, in High Peak we are indebted to Alistair Bunting from the County Council for investigating complaints of obstruction to rights of way and for achieving their restoration and repair, and to Will Steel, the Parish Paths Liaison Officer.

At the close of 1995 the following parishes had signed Partnership Agreements: Castleton, Chapel en le Frith, Charlesworth, Chisworth, Edale, Hayfield, Hope, New Mills and Whaley Bridge.

One wonders what will happen in Glossop or Buxton where there is no town council to instigate a path survey. It may well be that groups of the Rambler's Association become signatories of the Parish Paths Agreement and take responsibility for definitive footpaths.

In several parishes the Ramblers have already given assistance. For example, within New Mills Denzil Hallam from the RA worked with the Town Council, co-ordinated the survey and identified sites where path and sign erection was vital. After the Town Council had submitted costs to the PPP Liaison Officer, a grant of three thousand pounds was forthcoming, enabling the requisite furnishings to be installed. The High Peak Bridle Ways Association has a P3 agreement, enabling its members to purchase gates and signs for erection on the Borough's bridle ways.

Under the Parish Paths Partnership, or P3, the survey of paths requires that each right of way be broken down into a link. A link being that length of path between junctions with other paths or a road. Adjacent to New Mills, the P3 survey in Whaley Bridge identified 160 links among the 102 rights of way. Here 103 sign posts are required. The way forward in this parish lies in the creation of two circular walks and the provision of good stiles and signs along their routes.

Assuming that this Partnership is adopted by every parish within High Peak, we should, over the next three years, have all the rights of way surveyed, signed, waymarked and adequately stiled.

The Ten Church Challenge: a circuit walk

The Uniting Church at Whaley Bridge, occupying the former Methodist Church premises on Buxton Road, celebrates its Tenth Anniversary during Autumn 1996. The Church is central to a circuit of 10 chapels distributed around the Black Brook, Goyt and Todd Brook valleys. An inter-church walk has evolved linking these places of worship and this 21 mile route is fast becoming an annual autumn event. Variety is added by alternating the route – in some years it runs from Whaley Bridge to Whitehough and makes Kettleshulme the final chapel; another year Kettleshulme is the first port of call and Whitehough the last.

Here the route of the Ten Church Challenge, also known as The Circuit Walk, is described commencing from Whaley and heading out to Whitehough and Chinley. The walk breaks into short lengths, ending at places where buses or trains return weary walkers to Whaley. During the annual walk, the chapels provide ramblers with refreshments.

21

Whaley Bridge to Whitehough

Two and a half miles walking on roads, lanes and rough tracks.

Dark Peak Map required.

The walk begins from Market Street in the centre of Whaley Bridge, A5002, beside which are bus stops at the Jodrell Arms and the railway station. Walk south, passing shops and the Mechanics Institute, until the road curves and crosses the Goyt. On the right stands the Co-op, a little further along and opposite, stands the Uniting Church.

The first Wesleyan Society in Whaley Bridge dates from 1807. A Sunday School was established in the corn mill beside the River Goyt on Bridge Street. A preaching room was established in a former barn along Chapel Street behind the Post Office. With 365 scholars on the school register, new premises were required. The foundation stone of the Buxton Road school room was laid in 1821, and a seven hundred seat chapel was opened alongside on Thursday September 17th, 1868. The Tenth Anniversary celebrates the union of the Whaley Bridge Methodists with their United Reform counterparts.

On the left, between the Church [012811] and the railway bridge, turn into an industrial estate. This is Gisbourne Yard, named after the Gisbourne family who owned Whaley Bridge Colliery. The mine shaft, sunk in 1815, was called Waterloo Pit and stood on the site of the church car park. During the working life of the pit surplus hot water was supplied to the Wesleyans to heat their chapel. By turning right then left, a drive rises up between the industrial units to Caldene Terrace. Turn left, passing the houses and walking the line of the former Cromford and High Peak Railway. Old Road is met at

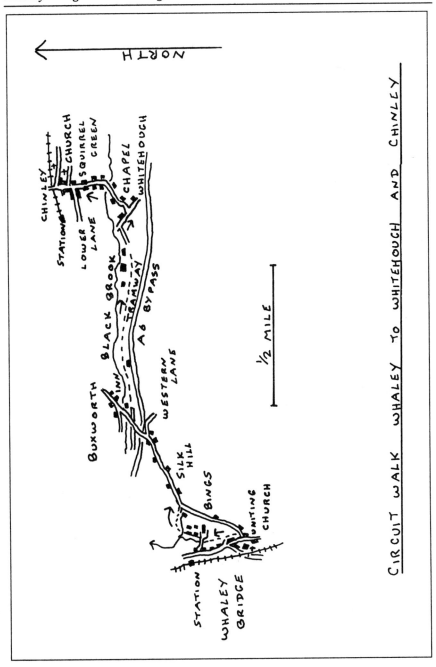

CIRCUIT WALK WHALEY TO WHITEHOUGH AND CHINLEY

Old Turns. Looking east up Bings Road, notice the tall building behind the garage, this was a ventilation shaft from the colliery.

Walking north across Old Road enter a wide surfaced track, this was a section of the C. & H.P. Railway and in a few yards it descends to George Street. Dating from 1832, this was a horse-powered incline working until 1952. In its latter days it was used to lower waggons of coal from the Buxton line to the Goyt Mill, which stood beside the Goyt where Woodbrook housing estate now stands.

At the bottom of the incline, walk across to Woodbrook [013815]. Note the bridge where Bridge Street crosses the Goyt, it was here the Roman Road from Manchester to Stockport and Buxton crossed the river. Here, when the Goyt was a divide between Derbyshire and Cheshire, stood the original Whaley Bridge. A seat made from the timbers of the original bridge survives in the Mechanics Institute.

Walk the path in the passage between Woodbrook and the river side wall. Observe that downstream of the road bridge, a restored rail bridge stands on the Cromford and High Peak Tramway, a metal switch point surviving from days when waggons were diverted into the Goyt Mills.

Walking the passage leads towards another set of mills, Bingswood. The passage turns away from the river, passes behind the houses to a metal kissing gate then proceeds up a tarmac path to Bings Farm and out onto Bings Road at a phone box and footpath sign. Walk north along Bings Road, noting the V.R. post box in the wall on the right. This narrow road leads past the houses onto the crest of Silk Hill, ahead are views up the Black Brook Valley. Trains speed up to Chinley and Sheffield, the by-pass carries traffic and on the valley floor, close to the stream, lies the Peak Forest Canal, its terminal basins reaching up to the Navigation Inn. Descend past the former hamlet of Gnat Hole, join Western Lane, formerly Weston Lane, cross the A6 by-pass and descend to the canal bridge. Cross the basin complex [022821]. After many years of restoration, it anticipates being re-opened on the bicentennial date in August 1996.

From the car park in front of The Navigation, turn up the valley and exit out of the car park's left-hand corner. Follow a tarmac road laid on the bed of the Peak Forest Tramway. The Black Brook lies to the left. A stone bridge carries a higher level tramway, a spur off the main line, running to village centre lime kilns.

The houses at Broken Bank are passed and it is possible to find a blank mile stone, one of many erected to measure the distance from the Peak Forest Canal's origin at Dukinfield Junction to Dove Holes. Nearer to a wooden footbridge there are the stone sleepers laid to support the short lengths of cast iron rail.

The tramway, now a rough road, reaches P.V.C. at Stephanie Works. To the left there black swans on the mill lodge. At the first road crossing turn uphill, passing homes on the left. Note the well in the opposite wall. On the left, at Sheridan House, take the passage beside the Old Hall Inn. Follow the passage to the far side of the inn. Opposite stands Whitehough Primitive Methodist Chapel and Sunday School, dating from 1840 [039821]. There are services every Sunday morning.

No public transport runs through Whitehough so continue into Chinley, a further half mile, for buses back to Whaley Bridge- not on Sundays.

22

Whitehough to Chinley

Half a mile on well-surfaced roads.

Dark Peak Map useful.

From Whitehough Chapel, descend Whitehough Head Lane, pavement on the left-hand side. At the bottom of the hill the Peak Forest Tramway crosses the lane. Victory Hall, used by the Scout Association, stands on the right. Cross the bridge over Black Brook [041822] and begin the ascent of Green Lane.

Ahead is the dramatic skyline of Cracken Edge on the slopes of Chinley Churn. As the centre of Chinley is approached, Lower Lane runs in from the left. Pass Squirrel Green on the right and The Squirrels. Finally turn right into Buxton Road. Chinley Chapel stands across the road [041827].

Victory Hall, which was passed earlier, was constructed in 1904 as St. John's, a chapel of ease from the mother church of St. Thomas A' Beckett, Chapel en le Frith. As a place of worship it survived until 1926/27 when it closed and ownership reverted to the Hadfields, owners of Forge Mills. After the Second World War, on December 4th 1947, it was given to the people of Chinley and Whitehough as a village hall, hence the name Victory Hall. The Scouts have had use of it since October 1977.

Chinley was known as Four Lane Ends, evolving around the junction of Green Lane, Stubbins Lane, Lower Lane and Buxton Road. By the year 1862, a Wesleyan preaching house capable of seating 80 worshippers in an upstairs room stood on Green Lane.

The railway provided the impetus for Chinley to develop and

enlarge. The first railway linking the village to the outside world was constructed by the Midland Railway Company. Chinley Station opened in February 1867 on a line constructed from New Mills to Millers Dale via Chapel en le Frith. The completed line served to join Manchester to Matlock, Derby and London. In 1894 the railway through the Hope Valley, linking Chinley to Sheffield via the Cowburn and Totley tunnels, was completed and the original Chinley station was pulled down. A new station was built to the west with six platforms and enjoyed being a major interchange for passengers travelling to and from Manchester, Stockport, Sheffield and London.

The line to Sheffield was widened in 1901. At New Smithy, east of Chinley, stood a Wesleyan day school. This school was demolished to enable the track work to commence. The building was taken down and rebuilt on Buxton Road, the stone laying ceremony taking place on June 30th 1901. It was decided to build a new chapel alongside. Looking at the Chinley Methodist Church today, we see the line of foundation stones dating from May 23rd. 1903. The chapel opened for worship in May 1904. Services are held every Sunday morning.

From Chinley an infrequent bus service, not Sundays, runs to Whaley Bridge and Buxton. Trains at a 2 hour frequency run to Manchester and Sheffield.

23

Chinley to Whiteknowle

One-mile, walking on pavement, farm track and footpath.

Dark Peak map useful.

From the Chinley Chapel on Buxton Road, turn east. Opposite stands St. Mary's Church with a foundation stone dated September 28th. 1907 and a Roll of Honour on the wall. Follow Buxton Road, pass Alpha Road and cross the culvert taking Otter Brook under the road. At the footpath sign turn left into Alders Lane [044826]. The lane passes houses before going under the railway track. On the far side of the railway Alders Lane continues across the fields, passing the house on the right, Otter Brook.

The lane descends to cross the Otter Brook and rises to a fork in the track. On the right is The Alders [047831]. Leave the lane by a narrow squeeze stile at the end of the garden wall.

Go into the field and follow the right-hand hedge to a stile in the corner bushes. Heading east, rise up the field to a wall corner. From the corner follow the wall to a gap in the next wall with a remnant of a stile. Aim to the farm building. Cross to the tall trees and locate a walled lane leading to a gate which gives access to the yard at White Knowle Farm. Following the drive to the right, exit the yard, pass the farm house and take the track ending at a footpath sign on Hayfield Road, A624. Turn down hill one hundred yards to Whiteknowle Chapel [051828].

The chapel, established 1809, has a Good Shepherd window. Look at the cenotaph. One side remembers the "Boys of Whiteknowle Chapel", on the reverse the "Boys of Chinley Wesleyan Chapel and Sunday School".

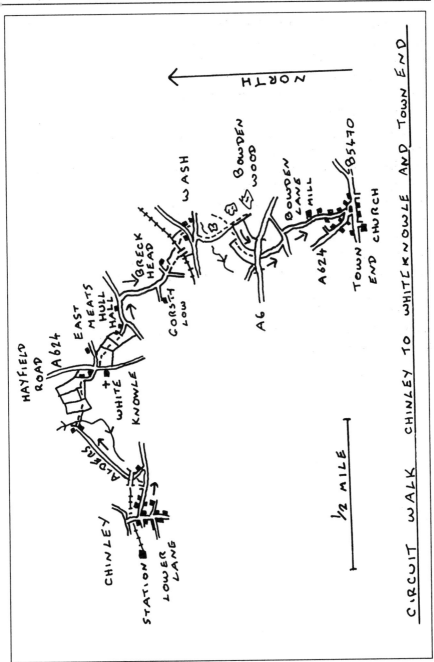

CIRCUIT WALK   CHINLEY TO WHITEKNOWLE AND TOWN END

Chinley was visited by John Wesley on several occasions, often accompanied by the local evangelist John Bennett. As Chinley became a recognised preaching place, a widow by the name of Goddard and her four children worked each Friday night at winding bobbins and their earnings were used to purchase tea as a drink for visiting preachers.

The construction of Whiteknowle Chapel was sanctioned by the Methodist Conference of 1808. A local preacher, Ralph Harrison, provided monies for the upstairs gallery and his daughter funded the organ. Harrison lived down the road at Ainsworth House, New Smithy. Here a Wesleyan Sunday School was established and enlarged in 1868 and 1882. By the time Harrison died in 1871 there were 145 scholars on the register. It was this school that was pulled down in 1901 and rebuilt on Buxton Road, Chinley. Services are held at Whiteknowle on alternate Sunday afternoons.

From Whiteknowle the Circuit Walk continues to Town End. If Whiteknowle is the end of one's walk, Hayfield Road can be descended to New Smithy for a short road walk into either Chapel en le Frith or Chinley.

24

Whiteknowle to Town End

Two miles, walking field paths, woodland and tarmac lanes.

Dark Peak Map useful.

From Whiteknowle Chapel, walk up Hayfield Road until opposite White Knowle Farm drive. Opposite is a track. Take the stile comprising three stone steps found on the right before the track. This gives access to the field. Walk downhill, following the wall. Pass between hummocks and cross over the stream on a flag stone culvert. Rise to a gate and stile then walk to the barn end [054827].

Due north of here stands the farm at East Meats which was the childhood home of nonagenarian Rev. Dr. William Simpson, affectionately known as Uncle Willie. This preacher's biography details his years of Christian work and witness beginning in the Chinley Independent Chapel, and still continuing at Brierley Green on the outskirts of Buxworth.

Go through the wide, metal gate close to the barn, pass the converted building and walk on past the farm house at Hull End, reaching the road at a footpath sign.

Follow the road uphill, passing Hull Hall, to a cross roads. Go right, descend to a ford and rise to pass the drive of Gorsty Low [058824]. There are good views ahead over Chapel en le Frith, from the Ferodo chimneys to the parish church tower.

Continue along the road to Breckhead, On the left on the bend is a stone building and sign post. Walk into the yard and bear right, looking for a narrow wooden gate on the right from where a walled passage leads into the field. Go to the railway line. The railway is crossed on bridge 67. From the steps and handrail over the bridge, walk towards the road, bear left and follow the over head power line to a metal gate. Cross the road, go between stone stumps and a flagged path leads down to a lower lane [061821].

On joining this lower lane, go right and first left. A wide path leads to Bowden Woods. The path runs by a stream, crosses a footbridge then runs up through a long narrow belt of woodland. Half way through the wood a path crosses from left to right. At this juncture leave the wood and go through the stile on the right. Following the left-hand hedge leads to a stile in a bush with views across to the railway arches, Eccles Pike and A6 by-pass.

The path runs towards the fly-over and drops into Bowden Lane [059816] close to Black Brook, on the outskirts of Chapel Milton. John Wesley passed this way on Sunday April 28th, 1745: "At five I preached at Mill Town near Chapel en le Frith. The poor miller near whose pond we stood endeavoured to drown my voice by letting out the water which fell with a great noise. But it was labour lost; for my strength was so increased that I was heard to the very skirts of the congregation."

Follow Bowden Lane south east to reach a main road. Taking care, cross and re-join the further length of Bowden Lane. Walk forward to Bowdenhay Mill, cross the former Peak Forest Tramway and continue over Black Brook. Walk between bollards which prevent through traffic, and finally emerge on Hayfield Road at Cross Scythes Garage. Walk forward, passing the florists, onto Buxton Road. Turn right to reach Town End Church [061808].

Services are held at Town End each Sunday morning.

For a return to Whaley Bridge there are bus stops here used daily by both local and express buses on their frequent journeys linking Stockport to Buxton.

25

Town End to Bagshaw

Two and a half miles on farmland paths.

Dark Peak map useful.

John Wesley was 42 when he encountered the miller at Chapel Milton. His last visit to Chapel en le Frith came on Monday April 3rd, 1786. In his eighty third year, Wesley recorded in his journal, "About eleven I preached to a crowded congregation in the new house near Chapel en le Frith."

This new house, the Wesleyan preaching house, had been built in 1780 on the site of the present chapel. It was described as a square building with a gallery on three sides and a dated lintel over the door. Construction on the present Town End Chapel began in 1872 and the dated lintel still survives over a rear door. In the past four years the building has been refurbished, a new porch provides a coffee bar and meeting room. In the adjacent yard the former school has been converted into houses and named Wesley Court.

From Town End chapel go onto Buxton Road. Walking east leads past the zebra crossing, and a left turn beside the florists leads into Hayfield Road East. Turn right, noting the houses to the rear of The Pack Horse, this is Reddish View, dated 1878. Ahead, as Hayfield Road curves back onto the Buxton Road, [063809] stand two houses, 9 and 7. Take the passage between them, a red brick wall on the right. This leads to Reddish Vale. At the stone stump turn left to follow the chain link fence, then cross the bridge over Black Brook.

From the bridge go up into Sam Longson's haulage yard. Cross the yard and, aiming to the left of the fuel tanks, go onto the Peak Forest Tramway. Cross the tramway bed, go through a stile, and take the

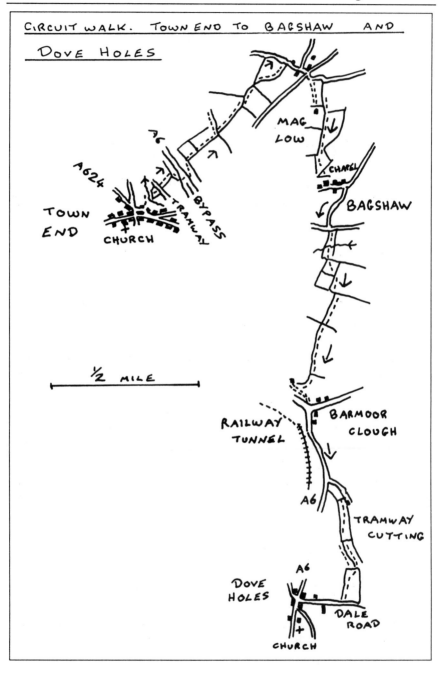

CIRCUIT WALK. TOWN END TO BAGSHAW AND DOVE HOLES

MAG LOW

CHAPEL

BAGSHAW

A624

TOWN END

CHURCH

BYPASS

TRAMWAY

A6

½ MILE

RAILWAY TUNNEL

BARMOOR CLOUGH

A6

TRAMWAY CUTTING

A6

DOVE HOLES

DALE ROAD

CHURCH

obvious path as it climbs up the field and reaches the lip of the by-pass cutting [066812].

Taking care, go right and follow the path which descends to the carriageway at the point where several lanes split. Again with great care, cross each of the split lanes and on the far side of the cutting wall ascend, until a kissing gate is met opposite the original path line. From the kissing gate follow the walls to trees, cross to the next wall and onto a narrow walled lane. Go over the ladder stile and follow the wall up the sloping pasture, aiming for a copse of trees on the summit. At the top of the pasture go through a stile on the right and up to the trees. From the copse [071817] follow the ridge top wall and pass through a gate with waymarks. The wall is followed downhill to another copse, through the gate and along a track to the tarmac road. Turn right, passing Keeper's Cottage, to Slack Hall Farm and the gates of the Chestnut Centre.

If time permits, go through the gates to view the Quaker graveyard [076819]. The dates on the gate posts are 1668 and 1862. Walk to the Castleton Road, where a Peak Park boundary millstone stands. Cross the road, enter the lane and go through a gate on the right. A public footpath sign is on the drive to Mag Low Farm. From here, climb up to the trees, skirt the fallen stone wall enclosing four sycamores, and look for a stile in the upper wall. Go over the wall, then follow it to the rear of the farm. Walk down to the fallen barns, keeping the wall on the right as far as the gorse bushes. The path does not go through the wall, it runs to the top of a wet gully where traces of a paved path remain [077812].

Descend the gully through the bushes on the left to a footbridge (concrete blocks make stepping stones). Go over a stile and descend from the footpath sign to a barn. Finally, drop down to the house, reach the road at the 'phone box and turn uphill, east, to the chapel [078811]. Bagshaw Wesleyan Chapel dates from 1886. Sunday afternoon services are held twice a month.

There is no public transport from here. Either continue to Dove Holes or take the road down the valley, passing Bagshaw Hall. Walk into the fields and a valley path heads down to the by-pass. Bus stops, served by local buses linking Stockport to Buxton, are found below the A6 by-pass on the Castleton Road.

26

Bagshaw to Dove Holes

Two and a half miles, paths, roads and tracks.

Dark Peak and White Peak Maps useful

From Bagshaw chapel go uphill to the junction and take the right turn. The road rises, giving wide views across the Bagshaw valley. Reach a T junction [078808] where a stile from the upper of two gates, opposite the junction, gives access to a path. This path follows the wall to a stream gully. At the gorse bushes, go over the small stream and head south over the rough pasture to a large stone stile. Walking in the same direction, cross to a corner stile in a rebuilt section of wall. Cross the wall into the upper field, heading for a bush and a wet gully. Across the wet patch there is a hurdle and stone stile. Go over and follow the wall on the right across a further stream. Pass from the Dark Peak to the White Peak Map and begin to move away from the wall so that you pass through the upper of two gateways. Following the wall past a muddy spring leads to a gate way. Ahead the railway can be seen running towards Dove Holes. A walled lane leads to a forking of tracks. At the dead tree above Higher Plumpton, go left down the grass bank onto the drive and descend to the junction at Barmoor Clough. Emerge at the confluence of A6 and A623 [078795].

From the road junction follow the A6 up Higher Hallsteads, walking off gritstone onto limestone. Those interested in the Peak Forest Tramway could cross the A6 here and scramble onto the former tramway bed close to the mouth of the 111 yard Barmoor Tunnel, on the Buxton railway line. Running close to the A6, a section of tramway bed can be discovered. The old stone sleepers remain in the grass. This is followed to the bridge and back onto the A6.

Continue along the A6 until the Dove Holes sign approaches. Before a bridge over the tramway bed, go left. In 100 yards on the right there is a green wagon. Go over a stile close to this wagon and cross the grass to the lip of a limestone cutting. On the cutting edge, aim towards a breeze block garage. Descend ten feet down the slope, contour to a point below the garage, spot the stile and descend to it, gaining the cutting floor [079788].

Back on the Peak Forest Tramway bed, follow it through a cutting of crinoidal limestone, looking for the stone sleepers which once supported the tramway rails. Continue to a stile, and fifty yards beyond go through a gate on the right. Follow the track by the trees [080781] to Dale Road. Once on the road, go west to the A6, and spot the Township of Fairfield stone. Reach the A6, go south away from the village, and cross Longridge Lane to find Dove Holes Chapel [076779]. The Primitive Methodist Chapel, erected 1876, has a foundation stone laid by Samuel Bibbington of Rochdale on August 19th. 1876. Services are held at Dove Holes each Sunday morning.

Dove Holes is served by trains running from Manchester to Buxton. Express and local buses stop in the centre of the village, at the end of Alexander Road.

27

Dove Holes to Combs

Three miles on roads, paths and tracks.

White Peak Map useful.

From the cross roads of Dale Road and Station Road with the A6, on the southern edge of Dove Holes, go west towards the railway. Just for a moment turn into Beech Lane on the left. Go to the end and look at the gable of the white-painted cottage on the left. A plaque on the wall says this was a Primitive Methodist Chapel, back in 1858. Return to Station Road and look in the garden wall for a boundary stone on the borders of Fairfield and Bowden Edge. Go up the road to the railway bridge, cross over the line and follow Meadow Lane. Fork left into Cowlow Lane [073783]. Continue rising past the houses, the final terrace stands on the right. Once in open country, the road dips slightly and there is a stile on the right.

Climb into the field, bear left to the wall and over the stile. To the north are the spoil heaps on top of the Dove Holes tunnel. Turning west, the path runs below the power line and crosses a second wall. The stile is a little distance from the gateway. Aiming for the trees at Cow Low Farm, go over a well- built stone stile and pass below the trees in front of the farm house. Pass the first projecting barn and turn right between the two buildings, then through a gate into the farm yard. Go left to pass the buildings, out of the stock yard and then turn right [067786]. Follow a track heading north, giving superb views over Chapel en le Frith.

To the left are the rounded slopes of Cow Low. Note the short section of wall. Go past the foot of this wall and skirt around the hill, following the 1250 foot contour. Close at hand is an air shaft on its spoil heap. The faint path crosses the head of Warmbrook Valley and reaches a wall.

Go over the stone stile and head for a gate and stile in a further wall [061786] then back onto Cowlow Lane by a stile close to the trees at the head of Ridge Clough. Once on the lane, go along the road and over the wall from the clough. Proceed for two hundred yards before turning down the track on the right, passing Ridge Hall and Ridge Farm [057789].

Continue down the track through the woods, pass Ridge Lodge and reach Chapel en le Frith station. Hourly trains run in the directions of Manchester and Buxton. Going onto Combs, cross the line [054795], but don't go through the opposite gate. Turn left and a path develops beside the line, which crosses Bank Hall drive. Continue along this path as it follows the line. After passing Owlgreave Farm, the path crosses the line,and, with the railway to the right, reaches Combs Lane [044788]. On the lane, go left passing The Avenue, left at the phone box, and first right into Ridge Lane. Pass the John Craven memorial seat. Opposite Pritchard Green Farm is the Wesleyan Chapel, dated 1864 [041784]. A monthly Sunday afternoon service is held in the chapel, and the building doubles as the village primary school and community hall.

There is no public transport out of Combs. To reach bus stops follow Combs Lane onto Manchester Road. At The Hanging Gate, there are frequent buses to Stockport and Buxton.

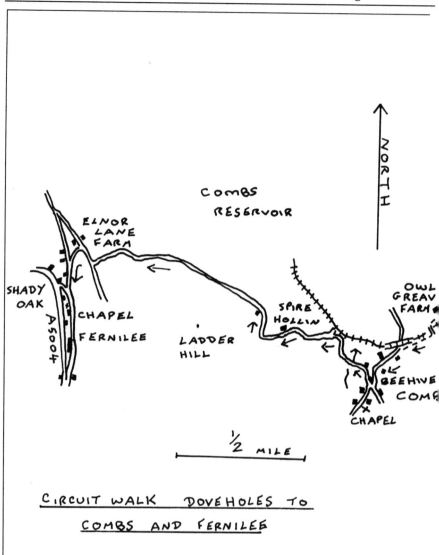

CIRCUIT WALK   DOVEHOLES TO
COMBS AND FERNILEE

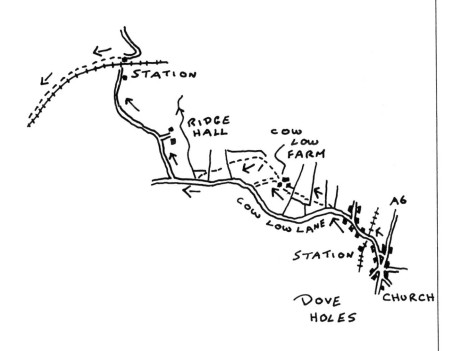

28

Combs to Fernilee

Two miles on roads and tracks.

White Peak Map useful.

From Combs chapel, return to The Beehive in the village centre. Turning right leads past the Post Office and down to the bridge over Meveril Brook. Ignore the fork at Quiet Ways and stay with the road to Collen Acre, looking back across the valley for the view to Castle Naze. The road passes Carr Green and climbs to Drovers End and Spire Hollin [034788]. Passing Spire Hollin the lane climbs again and meets a junction. Turn right, north, the tarmac is left behind; a stony road rises passing a barn, possibly a pack man's shelter. The track rises and gives views over Combs Reservoir, the railway at the foot of the hill, look beyond Eccles Pike to the distant Kinder plateau.

The rough road contours Ladder Hill at 1050 feet above sea level; to the north of the track, it fords a wet hollow where there was once a stone circle [023794], the standing stones long removed for building purposes. Reach the trees at Black Edge Plantation and walk down to Elnor Lane. Reach the route of the Roman Road linking Manchester to Buxton and go downhill towards Elnor Lane Farm. On the left is a rough surfaced walled lane; take this south to a tarmac road. A few minutes level walking leads past the cemetery to brick-built Fernilee Chapel dating from 1871 [017789]. This is close to the 900 foot contour; note the four initialled stones at each corner of the building. Services are held here each Sunday afternoon.

There is an infrequent bus service on weekdays from The Shady Oak back into Whaley Bridge, on Summer Sundays; several buses running to and from Buxton pass the pub. Elnor Lane leads downhill into Whaley Bridge.

29

Fernilee to Kettleshulme

Three miles, field paths, moorland and lanes.

White Peak and Stockport South map useful.

From the lane in front of Fernilee Chapel, go north, passing the cemetery at the end of the burial yard, Folds Lane leads down to Buxton Road, A5002. Just before reaching the Shady Oak, notice that you are crossing the line of the Cromford and High Peak Tramway. Cross Buxton Road [016790], and go down the track to the farm. There is a farm house on the left – go into the wide yard. There is a gate and stile straight ahead. The stile gives access to grazing land sloping down towards the River Goyt. Head forward and two gates can be seen. Ignore these, but look for a stile with white-painted posts behind a clump of nettles. Over the stile, descend down a tongue of land between two gullies. At the lower end of the left-hand gully there is a footbridge, cross the bridge, and go over a stile head to the river bank, aiming for Peak and Northern Footpath Sign 237. Cross the Goyt at Hillbridge [011787].

Go over the river, and through a stile on the right into the Derbyshire Wildlife Trust Hillbridge Reserve. There is a good chance of spotting deer in the next two miles.

Through the wood, the path rises into open pasture land. A wide, obvious path skirts Park Wood then crosses rough pasture to join Whitelease Road. Go right. Take the lane through the gate at Widow Clough and continue to Glebe Farm on the right. Go through the gate opposite or over the stile, avoiding an early bath. Climb up the field, following the wall. Go through a stile, up the next wall side and then over two stiles in quick succession. The climbing now stops, and

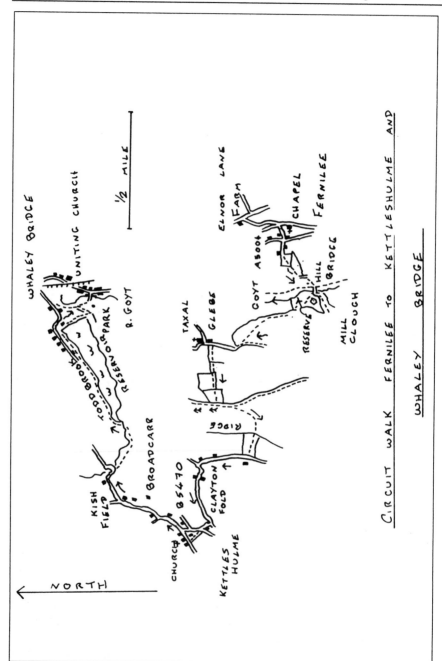

CIRCUIT WALK FERNILEE TO KETTLESHULME AND

WHALEY BRIDGE

there is level walking across the field to a ladder stile on Taxal Edge Road [001797].

On the road go left, south, to the end of the wood. A track leaves the road and climbs up through sparse rhododendrons. You are now in the parish of Hartington Upper Quarter. Reach a notch in Taxal Edge [997793], and views stretch over most of this Circuit Walk. Over the ridge, at 1100 feet above sea level, the walk enters Cheshire. Climb a stile into Kettleshulme parish. There are views ahead across the Todd Brook Valley, notice white-painted Bow Stones Farm on the skyline. Aim ahead for white-gabled Wrights Farm, join Higher Lane and turn north, right.

Follow the lane past Lapwing Farm to Green Head Farm then go left, down past Clayton Fold [994799]. Note the plaque above the farm house door.

A barking dog once discovered a baby boy hidden in a bush. Because of the dog's barking the foundling was called "Ouffe". He was christened Thomas. In 1610 Thomas Ouffe married Anne Rowe, and by 1624 they occupied Clayton Fold Farm. He died four years later and was buried at Prestbury. The executors of his estate set up a charitable trust providing monies for the poor of six villages and the salary of a schoolmaster. The school was down Elnor Lane at Shallcross. Ouffe's Bequest is still administered.

From Clayton Fold follow the lane which runs between fields until it drops to Flatts Lane, Kettleshulme. Turn right, passing Bank Terrace, dated 1880. Note the swan wind vane on the pub roof. Join Macclesfield Road, B5089, pass The Swan, and turn in through the gates of the garden centre. Follow the track through the nursery, pass below the lych gate and reach Kettleshulme Chapel [988799].

Among the first Wesleyans at Kettleshulme were George Brockle-hurst and John Boothby. Worship was held at Billinge Brow, Rai-now, in the Macclesfield Circuit. A preaching house was established in 1808 on Higher Lane, now Chapel House Farm. The village centre church opened on June 15th. 1815, three days before the Battle of Waterloo. The building fell into decay and closed in 1899. Whilst funds were being raised, the congregation met in Lumbhole Mill.

The chapel was restored, new foundation stones date from June 11 1901. The church opened in October 1901. In recent months the church has once again raised funds for a major refurbishment of the chapel. Services are held each Sunday afternoon.

Three buses a day link Kettleshulme to Macclesfield and Whaley Bridge.

30

Kettleshulme to Whaley Bridge

Two miles, walking on lanes, in woodland and on parkland.

Stockport South Map useful.

From Kettleshulme chapel, go left out of Paddock Lane into Kishfield Lane [989800]. The lane passes Well House and Greenlands, dated 1754. Continue downhill past Hardy Green. Ignore the drive to Broadcarr, but continue past Colehurst to Kishfield Farm and down to the bridge over Todd Brook.

On the right before Todd Brook there is a stile, go over, enter a birch copse and discover Peak and Northern sign post 264 [994807]. Take the Whaley Bridge route. The path rises to the rim of the woods and runs level on a high path above the meandering stream. Enjoy views through the trees across to Scar Wood, then go down to the banks of Todd Brook. Continue down stream to the massive stone steps and follow the reservoir by-wash through the woods [999807].

If the Todd Brook is in flood, it will not be possible to cross the stream at the top of the weir. Instead locate a path several hundred yards upstream which contours above the pine trees onto Walker Brow. Exit through Walker Farm onto Macclesfield Road and go down the road to Reddish Avenue on the left. This is followed to Reddish Farm and Toddbrook Reservoir.

Normally, crossing the Todd Brook takes the route back into Derbyshire and out of the National Park. The path follows the by-wash, through the trees on the right the reservoir is visible. After two remote homes and the Topper Fox memorial seat, a bridge is crossed [003808]. Here the stream is split, a portion floods into the reservoir and the remainder by-passes the dam en-route to the River Goyt.

The path reaches the dam. It may be possible to cross the apron of the side weir. If not, join Reservoir Road and cross the bridge onto the dam at Todd Brook Lodge [007812]. Walk across the dam, built 1836 – 1839 by the Peak Forest Canal Company to supply the canal at Whaley Bridge with water. Across the dam a stone stile is met and the Midshires Way joined. Turn left, following the path between hedge and fence into the park. The path becomes tarmac surfaced. Go down the slopes below the cenotaph and cross the bridge over the Goyt [011809]. This leads you up Wheatsheaf Road onto Buxton Road, and a left turn leads past The Cock, below the railway and back to the Uniting Church.

Return to Whaley Bridge having either done the Ten Church Challenge as one day's hike or having spread the miles over several days. I think people would agree that they have seen some little-visited corners and communities within the Borough of High Peak.

The historical aspects of this Circuit Walk have been gathered from the booklets of Alan Watson and material supplied by Hazel Senior and Arthur Jackson.